How to make a killing in PENNY SHARES

by

Michael Walters

Dear Friend,

Like myself, Michael Walters has a passion for Penny Shares. I hope that reading this book infects you with the same enthusiasm we both have for the most exciting shares on the stock market. Enjoy this great introduction to Penny Shares, with my compliments.

Good luck,

Tom Winnifrith

 ISBN 1 899964169

How to make a killing in PENNY SHARES

by

Michael Walters

Laddingford Books

Tel: 01892 730231

Other books by Michael Walters:

How to Make a Killing in the Alternative Investment Market

How to Make a Killing in the Share Jungle

How to Make a Killing in New Issues

DO NOT READ THIS BOOK

* If you do not understand that the stock market is a dangerous place where you can lose all of the money you have put into it.

* If you do not want to gamble in one of the riskiest sectors of the stock market.

* If you are content to leave the biggest stock market winners to others, and to miss an awful lot of fun.

CONTENTS

PAGE

Introduction

✷

Penny shares can be pure magic, the answer to an investor's prayer. Anyone enjoying the great internet revolution which really started to hit the stock market in the autumn of 1999 will know they can multiply your money one hundred-fold in a matter of days. Or, in the case of the Archie Norman backed shell company Knutsford, in a matter of hours. Penny share opportunities have always been there. Polly Peck went from 9p to £36 in the Eighties. Pentland Industries soared from 20p to £30 a few years later. Around the New Millennium, the action has just come faster, and more frequently. How can you resist it?

When the market is in a confident mood, penny shares can, and often do, transform a gamble of a few hundred pounds into a healthy investment worth several thousands. They can make small investors into quite large investors in a matter of months. Watch out, though. When the market turns bad, or you simply get it wrong, penny shares can cost you a lot of money quickly. Floated at a few pence, Knutsford hit 275p late in 1999, and had slumped to 125p by February. Even then, many thought there was further to fall. But you never really thought the stock market was safe, did you?

It has been bonanza time through the winter of 1999 and towards spring 2000. As the internet revolution has brought private investors the opportunity of instant access to company information, and the ability to swap ideas over internet bulletin boards, individual investors have been roaring into action. And one internet-linked company after another has soared to score massive gains. Investors large and small have been multiplying their money many tunes over in a matter of weeks.

The gains have been breath-taking, and many of them have been in penny stocks. It has long been that way. Though the Nineties began in grim, sober mood, many penny shares doubled, trebled, and quietly quadrupled in the early years. Through the mid-Nineties, there were big winners galore, though not quite in the stratospheric style of the Eighties. And the momentum gathered towards the end of the decade. If you got your stock and timing right, you could have done wonderfully well.

Suddenly, towards the end of 1999, it all took off. Small investors poured into the market, attracted by tales of soaring share prices. Soon, the City pages were carrying complaints about how long it took to contact brokers on the phone. Individuals began threatening legal action if they had to wait for more than 30 minutes, and missed the chance of making a few thousand because they could not buy in time.

Have no doubt that the stories are real. In an earlier edition of this book in November 1998, after a sharp setback in share prices, I was still able to spot massive penny winners. At that stage, you could see Calluna up from 7.5p to 24p, Rage Software from 4p to 10p, GTL Resources from 4p to 11.75p, Dentmaster from 2.75p to 5p, Dimension Resources warrants from 3.5p to 17.5p. And so on.

Doing the exercise again at the beginning of March 2000, and you are embarrassed for choice. Take the two share pages of the *Financial Times*, run down the columns of highs and lows for the previous twelve months, and you will grow dizzy with delight. There are gains galore, and massive ones. Just to pick a few, you can find Amstrad up from 42.75p to 568p, Tepnel Life Sciences from 10.5p to 127p, AIM Trust from 68.5p to 508p, Aortech from 86p to 835p, Tardis from 12p to 1110p, e-capital from 1.75p to 41p, eVestment from 2p to 48p, Oxford Biomedica from 17p to 130p, West 175 from 43.5p to 480p, Medisys from 16p to 120p, Minmet from 6.5p to 46p. And so it goes on.

You had to be lucky, very lucky to spot them? Maybe. Or perhaps you simply had to keep your eyes open. By no coincidence at all, I tipped every single one of those shares in that twelve month period, either in *The Daily Mail* or in one of the other places where I write about shares. So a few million people had access to many of those ideas.

Do not get me wrong. I am not claiming that I spotted them all at the very bottom. But I came pretty close with one or two. And anyone following my tips would have multiplied their money five, ten, fifteen times or more – though I should admit that I did pretty nearly as well with a smaller number of higher value stocks. One stock I picked in March 1999 was stockbroker cum internet investment trust Durlacher. Recommended at the equivalent to 92p, it touched £40 early in 2000. In fairness, though, that did not start out as a penny share. There were capital changes along the way – but the gain was real.

It was a fantastic period, the run from 1999 into the first quarter of 2000. It might not happen again. But ... who knows ? That is part of the thrill of it.

And it could be you, riding a monster winner, gambling in penny shares. There were many other penny shares which went up five-fold or more in the course of 1999. Perhaps it was an exceptional year, an extraordinary one. But when the time is right, the gains can be dramatic. Look at an earlier escapade.

In May 1995, Queens Moat Houses returned to market after two years in limbo. The hotels group had survived massive losses and a major reconstruction. When dealings re-started, millions of shares were traded for as low as 3p on the opening day. From the peak, that was equivalent to a fall from 475p to 3p. Shattering stuff.

That, though, created an opportunity if you were alert. A friend helped me through the arithmetic, and it became clear that Queens Moat shares might be grossly undervalued. I decided they should feature in my *Daily Mail* investment column. By the time I wrote the piece, on a Thursday, the price had doubled to 6.25p. When it appeared in print, the price was 9.25p, with 40 million or so shares changing hands each day.

Almost at once, the price roared away to touch 18.5p. On the next day, the Tuesday, it touched 21p. At that stage it attracted the attention of professional bear raiders, market experts who try to make money by selling shares they do not have in the hope of buying them more cheaply later. By the end of the week, Queens Moat were back to 13p. In the weeks which followed, they traded down to 9.75p, but kept swinging around quite sharply.

In fact, Queens Moat proved to be a dream stock for the alert penny punter. It kept bouncing up, and falling down. In the first ten months of 1998, it touched extremes of 12.25p and 43.75p. It is hard to guess what the correct value might be. But that is an illusion. There is no "correct" value – only what the market will pay.

The story shows what can happen if you get a penny share at the right moment. It was no narrow market stock – hundreds of millions traded in the course of a week in May 1995. In theory, you could have bought at 3p and sold at 21p, a seven-fold gain in four trading days – though I doubt that anyone did that well. You could have made three times your money by getting your timing right between extremes in 1998.

The tale is also worth telling because it illustrates that, when it comes to spotting an opportunity, this is not an example of being wise after the event. It was an exceptional case, but anyone could play. There was no secret. The evidence was there as it happened, for millions of *Mail* readers to make up their own mind. Penny shares really can be something special.

If you are thinking of tiptoeing into penny shares in the New Millennium, the odds may be in your favour. Companies large and small – like Queens Moat – were still collapsing or going to the brink in 1993. Far fewer fell by the wayside in 1994, hardly any in the following years. By the late Nineties, the crippling impact of the strength of sterling set some worrying. And the small companies sector, where most penny shares are to be found, did have a dull period.

They came bounding back to life in 1999. There were still a few worries. Calluna, for example, is suspended as I write, and the future looks grim. It was a great punter favourite for a while through 1998 (though not for me). And some of the older, bigger name businesses whose shares had drifted down to penny share status also fared badly. Look through the High Street names, and some are limping along. Furniture retailer UNO is struggling as I write, Bhs and Mothercare giant Storehouse looks as if it will be rescued by a takeover bid, toy shop group Era is drifting down. And so on. Gradually rising interest rates as we go into 2000 will not help.

There are no guarantees, but the chances of making a killing in penny shares are alive again as we move through the late Nineties. The shrewd or simply lucky penny players really can multiply their money eight – nine – or ten-fold in a year or two when conditions are right. It does happen. I have done it myself.

Whenever I speak at investment conferences, I never mind the questioner who asks why, if I know so much, I am not rich, and wants to know how well I have done trading shares. Quite right.

Financial journalists are not lavishly paid, and my personal circumstances have meant I have always been short of capital. In addition, I have set down strict conditions under which I can buy and sell shares, quite properly making sure that I trade ethically and put the interests of readers before my own. So, while I have the advantage of being constantly in touch with the news, my own trading is actually placed at a significant disadvantage in many ways.

One real-life example is especially worth recounting. In April 1983, I bought shares in a company called Applied Holographics. I knew a little about holograms from my interest in high technology companies, which had started when I visited the wild, woolly and terrifying American penny stock market then ablaze in Denver. Watching the extraordinary ups and downs there prompted me to start reading popular science magazines to try to understand a little more. From that, I knew holograms had remarkable potential. A sort of three dimensional picture, they could be used in advertising and as security printing and information storage devices. They pop up now as the sparkling, silvery patch in the corner of most credit cards.

I had been out of the country for a few weeks. Catching up on the financial pages when I returned, I noticed something called Applied Holographics was to be floated on the over-the-counter market in London. United Trust & Credit, a relatively new corporate finance business whose directors had a reasonable record, were sponsoring the issue.

I got a copy of the prospectus, read it carefully, and decided that this untried venture would either make a fortune, or go bust fairly quickly. The United Trust people were struggling for recognition, though, and needed to get their early issues right. It seemed too risky to recommend to readers, but I decided to take a gamble myself, and put a few hundred pounds in.

The issue was oversubscribed, so I did not get all of the shares I wanted. I bought more in the small over-the-counter market, placing particular emphasis on the warrants – the lowest-priced, most highly speculative pieces of paper.

Two years later, I sold a large part of my holding. The company was still struggling, but had gained a quotation on the Stock Exchange. Although the debut had been disappointing, my shares were up seven-fold. My warrants had rocketed, some thirty-fold, others ten-fold. My few hundred pounds was worth several thousand.

I have not told this story in some feeble attempt to impress with my investment skills. For what it is worth, the cash I made repaired a hole dug by an earlier unfortunate speculation (not in a penny stock). Over the years, I have made big profits, and hefty losses. I hope I have learnt from my mistakes, and my winners. But when I write about investment, I do it with experience as both a winner and a loser, not as some academic, theoretical analyst.

Experience in the real world is a big advantage when it comes to share dealing. It plays an important part in the tipping column I have been writing in the *Mail* for many years, where my winners and losers are on display. I believe it makes a telling contrast with tipping services which carry no name, or just a pseudonym. You do not know who contributes, nor what their experience might be. It also contrasts with some who suggest that financial journalists should not buy shares. I believe quite the opposite. Only those with experience of what really happens in the share market should be allowed to tip shares. Would you take driving lessons from someone who had only read the manual?

Applied Holographics, by the way, struggled through the Nineties. But in November 1998, years after I had sold my stake in the company, it appeared to me that it could be on the brink of a big breakthrough. I recommended it in my *Mail* investment column. Fingers crossed. In 2000, it is booming, though the name has been changed to Applied Optical.

My experience with Applied Holographics in the Eighties means I really do know how a small investor can make big winnings in penny stocks. It is also worth recounting because it illustrates several of the things which can help in finding a winner. I spotted the opportunity by taking the trouble to keep in touch with events. Reading back copies of newspapers after weeks away can be a real chore – but it can be important. And, even for a financial journalist, it shows what a useful source of investment ideas the newspapers can be.

Equally, I had spent time trying to learn a little about new high technology developments, because I thought there might be an opportunity there. It paid off. While I did not know enough to evaluate Applied Holographics in depth (after I bought the first shares, I bought a textbook on making holograms, and gave up after page 35, baffled), I had picked up enough to recognise that there might be something interesting.

Those who followed my tipping column in the mid-Nineties might have guessed I spent time reading up on computer companies and the information superhighway. I am still struggling to understand it, but doing some homework helped me make several outstanding tips (including a four- or five-fold winner inside nine months for any who took my advice on backing internet service provider Unipalm).

It always helps to know something about the background of the house sponsoring the issue. In the Applied Holographics case, I could be reasonably confident of the track record of the sponsors, and knew their need to succeed ensured their commitment to the company – though they fell apart in the troubles of the late Eighties.

And I went in for a relatively small amount of money, knowing it was cash

I could afford to lose, but that if it came right, the return could be very good. I deliberately weighted my investment towards the highest-risk form of the shares (the warrants), and resisted opportunities to snatch a quick profit while the shares kept rising in the limited over-the-counter market. Only when the shares were trading on a proper market and began to slip back did I start to sell. Had I held on for a couple of years longer, I would have done better still – but my Applied Holographics profits gave me a bigger stake to spread my risk and play other stocks.

In fact, I did not find another performer to match Applied Holographics in the Eighties, though they were there. Others spotted them. My high-risk investment policy later brought me a couple of total losses, a few heavy losers, and some brilliant gains, which far outweighed the setbacks. Many were in penny stocks. One went up forty-fold, though I was not clever enough to sell more than a few shares near the very top. All of my ventures have involved pretty small stakes, but in the end they mean that I now have a useful cushion of savings – something I would never have had without playing the share game. It is beginning to transform my life as I grow older.

Make no mistake, though. There are snags to the penny share game. The great stock market crash of October 1987 hammered small companies, and penny shares in particular. Over the next year, many fell to a quarter or less of their peak value – though the gains had been so good that many punters were still ahead even then.

After October 1987 it became still harder to buy or sell in reasonable quantities at fair prices. By the early Nineties, perhaps 100 public companies had gone bust. Not all were penny share companies – they never got big enough to over-borrow so much – but there were many penny casualties.

Penny stocks are the wild ones, the stock market gambling counters. Just as the chances of seeing a substantial gain in a penny stock are much greater than with shares selling for a few pounds, so the chances of taking a nasty tumble are much greater. But there is nothing which says you cannot sell and get out of the game when it turns rough. Do that, and you can avoid the worst, and salvage some of your stake money.

No matter what the authorities might pretend, the Stock Exchange is much like a casino. In my book *How To Make A Killing In The Share Jungle* I open with the message "Safer than the 3.30 at Chepstow, more fun than the football pools, better than breaking the bank at Monte Carlo – a fortunate few make millions playing the stock market every year, some by luck, some by judgement. Anyone can play. You may not make the millionaire club, but even the most modest investors can multiply their money many times over. You, too, can make a killing in the share jungle."

That raised a few eyebrows, but nothing I have heard during nearly 40 years as a financial journalist, watching the City at work and play, has prompted me to change that judgement. If anything, the stock market is more like a casino than ever.

The Stock Exchange odds, though, are weighted more in favour of the punter than in any other form of gambling I know. Rarely do you lose all of your stake money – even in penny shares – so long as you stick to shares listed on the London Stock Exchange. And every day, all along the way, there is an opportunity of selling out, salvaging what chips you have left, and changing your bet.

The penny share jungle is simply rougher, tougher, and more exciting than the rest of the market. Do not enter unless you are prepared for thrills and spills, and can face the possibility of losing all your stake money. The risks are great, but the potential rewards are high. Though many established City names frown at playing the penny share game, and dismiss it scathingly, do not let them intimidate you. Your bank manager may not like it, your solicitor will shudder. Leave them to plod along.

Not every investor wants to play a conservative, conventional investment game. Not everyone wants a solid, blue-chip portfolio which will let them sleep easy at night. Many want a fling, to play for double or quits, and are quite prepared for an outright gamble. If you only have £1,000 or £2,000 and can afford to lose it, what point is there in earning a solid 10% return each year? Your 10% gain amounts to £100 or £200. Peanuts, really. What you need is a gamble, something which will make worthwhile winnings if you get it right.

It can happen. It does happen. All it needs is good luck – and perhaps a little good judgement. This book offers no guarantees – there are none in the penny share jungle. But it should help stack the odds in your favour. Good luck.

ONE

Penny Shares – the Pluses and the Problems

✸

Penny shares are the stock market mavericks, neglected by big league players, cast out by the establishment and often treated as rather rakish, not quite the thing for proper investors. At the same time, they can be what every investor wants – shares which will outperform the average, and can treble, quadruple, perhaps rocket ten-fold in the wink of an eye.

You know it makes sense. You are not reading this book because you want to play it safe and match the market averages, making or losing a trifling 10% or 20%, just like everyone else. You want something special, something which will add real punch to your portfolio if it works. You are ready to take the consequences, ready to risk the losses if you get it wrong. Forget staid City sniping, the vague notion that somehow it is not quite the respectable approach to investing. That comes from people who have not paused to think properly for themselves, who are happy to stick to what they think they know, what everyone tells them. Or who have a vested interest in persuading you to let them look after your money, providing them with a cosy meal ticket.

For the smaller investor, penny shares can offer the most realistic chance of a killing, of the investment break-through. Picking penny share winners can create the capital to move on to what are generally considered safer, more solid investments. Sadly, those sorts of "respectable" shares usually generate rewards which hardly seem worth the patience if you only have a small amount of capital in play. If punting penny shares resembles playing the football pools or the National Lottery without having to stake new money each week, fair enough. There is nothing wrong with that. The chances of making a tidy sum in penny shares are immeasurably better than the chances of winning the

Lottery or something worthwhile on the pools, though you hardly need to lay out much more stake money.

Penny shares offer an attractive way of speculating to accumulate, the chance of a short-cut to a sizeable share portfolio. So long as you go in with your eyes wide open, aware of the risks as well as the potential rewards, there is nothing to worry about. Sensible penny share players know the odds, and have no need to apologise to anyone for their investment strategies. They make every bit as much sense – maybe more – than the automatic, safety-first mantra many City advisers mutter as a matter of course. What happens if you are holding safety-first stuff when the whole market tumbles? You get sheared, along with the other sheep.

A prudent, commendable 10% return each year means little if you only have £500 or £1,000 to play with. What can you do with £50, or £100 these days? It is hardly going to change your life-style. Even a top-class 20% return counts for little more. Splash out on high-risk, high-return penny shares though, and that £500 or £1,000 might just push you into the big time. You could double it, treble it, even quadruple it. Or you might lose a large chunk of it. Winning would make a big difference. Lose, and you will be able to shrug it off, unless you have been very foolish. Either way, though, you need to look at the pluses, and the problems of penny shares.

The Top Performers

Penny share magic really does work. Time and again, penny shares crowd the top twenty when the tables of top performers are published. In most years, the majority of the best-performing shares started the year at less than 100p. The winnings vary, of course. But in a good year, the best of them have achieved enormous gains.

My introduction has listed some of the penny shares I followed in 1999, and which made staggering gains. Happily, many of those stocks were favourites with small investors. Most of them featured on the internet bulletin boards, where anyone with access to the internet can put up messages about any share they like. Within certain common-sense bounds, they can say what they like. And that has allowed investors to spot many massive winners.

The remarkable feature of this internet age has been the speed with which prices move. I tipped one stock, eVestment, to a group of investors early in

September at 3.25p. Eight weeks later, it was 48p. It soon fell away as it became apparent that some of the gossip reported in the financial press was wildly inaccurate, but the price did settle around 36p. Pretty sensational stuff, by normal standards.

It might not be fair to talk about the internet incubator companies which floated for 2p or 5p and went to 100p in a week or so – the likes of Jellyworks and Oxygen. Few small investors were able to buy them at the issue price. Even with these, though, startling gains were possible. Lucky timing could have put you into Jellyworks at 60p, and out at 120p in a few days.

And one of my perennial favourites, mining exploration group Minmet, went from 6.5p at the start of 1999 to 21p by the end of the year. Then to 46p in mid-February. As I write, a small bio-tech stock called Provalis has floored me. I was about to tip it, started my research with the price at 18.5p, and abandoned it when the price began to rise before I could get into print. Within a week, it was 46p. A similar thing happened with Proteome Sciences, another bio-tech baby. I began investigating at 55p, and a few days later it was all over the bulletin boards, and the price had topped 130p.

There have been countless examples in the sensational six months form September 1999 to March 2000. I have simply spotlighted a few which come immediately to mind. And though the internet excitement has touched some of these, and set even Chancellor Gordon Brown warning about share speculation, the small investor has been making hay. Anyone reading earlier editions of this book will find I was able to produce many examples from earlier years – not quite so many, and without such spectacular gains. But enough to emphasise that there are always winning opportunities in penny shares.

Forgive me for plugging some of my hits. There have been misses, but most of the loses have been kept relatively modest by following a stop-loss system. The main point in listing a few penny winners is to prove that they can be found and to demonstrate that this book is written by someone who practices what he preaches in print, where it can be judged by the 2.3m people who buy the *Daily Mail* each day.

When I say it can be done, I have proved it, in print. And sometimes by trading for myself – ethically, of course. There are dozens of investment writers who never mention whether they manage to pick winners themselves. And there are thousands of pundits – in the press, and around the City – who say it is easy to pick winners in a bull market, or among penny shares. Most trade with the benefit of hindsight. They will tell you they knew such and such a share was a goodie. My winners – and some losers – are there for all to see, as it happens. If I get it wrong – as I do, sometimes – there is no hiding. I have to face up to it in print, and apologise.

So when someone sneers at penny shares, shrug it off. The pounds you make in penny shares will buy just as much as any you might make backing blue chips. Though you are taking a gamble, the rewards could be brilliant.

Room to Grow

Obviously, penny shares do not beat the market every time. The biggest winnings listed above are in the vintage years of the penny share game, when the market was flying. When the market was on the slide, penny shares fared worse than the average. They fell further, and became more difficult to sell in reasonable quantities. But a good proportion of the big winners were still penny stocks.

When it comes to doing the arithmetic, penny shares have a whole lot going for them – an in-built advantage, thanks to their size and the volatility of their prices.

It is simple common sense: because penny share companies are generally smaller, newer, or weaker companies, they have more room to grow. There is no reason why penny share companies should be that way. There is no accounting reason why a giant like Boots or Marks & Spencer should not shuffle their structure so that their shares sell for a few pence each. It would mean creating vast numbers of new shares in a paper-juggling accounting exercise which would not change the real worth of the company. They will not do it. It just does not happen. Big companies and their big investors prefer chunkier shares – not too heavily-priced, but not too light.

Bigger, better-established companies simply do not grow at the pace of smaller ones.

Boots has done nicely, but with a market value of £4.3bn, it is unlikely to rocket. Marks & Spencer has a value of £7bn. If anything is to make that double, it will be a take-over. These companies are too big, too set in their ways, unless there is a complete transformation in the City's view of retailing.

Such things do happen from time to time. Marconi doubled in 1999 as it emerged from the old shell of GEC into a more exciting teleconus/technology opportunity. Vodafone Air Touch performed a similar feat by going out and buying business in a fashionable sector. Because the shares sell for relatively large amounts, it is asking quite a lot for them to rocket. Some have gone from £5 to £40 in a year or so – internet experts Durlacher, chip designer ARM and Israeli switch company BATM have actually done rather better – but they have had very compelling technology stories to tell. The average investor, though, does not feel good paying £10 for something which was £5 a few months earlier. The psychology is wrong.

In some cases, too, we have reached the point where the biggest businesses have simply grown too big to go anywhere fast. In the world of wheeling and dealing, the theme emerged most aggressively when Hanson Trust, the business Lord Hanson and Lord White built by buying other companies, selling bits, and beefing up others, made a successful bid for tobacco giant Imperial Group. Hanson would not be able to keep up the pace of expansion, it was argued, because there would soon be no companies big enough for them to take over. That would slow the pace of growth. Small deals would not make enough return. That, indeed, proved to be the truth for Hanson. Through the Nineties, Hanson shares lagged the market, until the management decided to break it into smaller units.

That was an extreme example, but the Nineties have brought management buy-outs galore. Quite large chunks of giant companies were sold to their managers, who nurtured them for a while, then brought them back to market, where they proved capable of growing more quickly on their own than as part of some wide-ranging giant.

And as we moved into the new century, scores of big companies found they had more cash than they knew what to do with. The vogue for companies to buy their own shares – shrinking their capital base – in order to speed the advance of earnings per share really took hold. More and more, bigger began to mean bogged down. The trend towards smaller units, though it was rarely presented as such, could be clearly recognised if you judged companies by what they did, rather than what they said they were doing.

Small is Beautiful

Smaller companies, and those with penny share prices, have no such concerns. They simply want to get bigger, faster. It is relatively easy to imagine some company boosting profits from £100,000 to £300,000 in one year – trebling growth with a flair even the genius of GUS could never match. It does not mean that the mini-company is remotely in the same class as GUS. But it does mean that the share price could easily treble – or more – in response to good news.

And it is not too off-putting for the private investor to toddle off and buy shares for 4p, even though they may have been selling for 1p a few months earlier. The real worth (whatever that may be) of the penny share company may not have changed at all, and may not warrant a three-fold increase in the stock market value. Investor perception is the key. But what does an extra 3p matter, when you think the shares may go to 10p? Never mind the quality, feel the width. The mere fact that someone thinks the shares are worth much more than they were may be measure enough of "real" worth. A thing is worth what someone will pay for it.

The Arithmetical Advantage

There is another arithmetical advantage, too, for the penny share punter. It may not quite be true to say that the sky is the limit for a low-priced share – but there certainly is a limit to the distance it can fall. The floor is not so far away.

It is obvious. Buy a share for 10p, and you cannot lose more than 10p on that share. In practice, unless it goes bust, you will almost always find you can sell it for 1p or .25p. That may sound derisory, but it is a larger proportion of your original stake than you might get back in a higher-valued dud – equivalent to 5p or 2p for a share which has fallen from 100p, and might go all the way down to 1p. Get it right, however, and you could make far more than 10p a share. If it trebles, you will make a profit of 20p, and your original 10p will be worth 30p. You could lose 100%, but you could make 200%. Or 1,000%, perhaps more.

This almost trite piece of arithmetic is worth thinking about. The odds are that you will not lose the whole of your 10p, whatever happens. There will almost always be a penny or two left. Though there was a flurry of collapses in the early Nineties, relatively few public companies go bust leaving shareholders with nothing, outside a recession. There could hardly have been a worse basket-case than Brent Walker. Yet for years through the mid-Nineties, it was still possible to sell the shares for a few pence, though in reality the debt they were carrying had made them worthless long before.

The most spectacular wipe-out of the late Nineties has come with Ionica, a company intended to exploit wireless telecommunications. Floated by SBC Warburg, one of the best-known City houses, it came to market in July 1997 at 390p. Soon afterwards, the shares touched 421p, a valuation of £640m. Yet by the end of October 1998, fifteen months after flotation, Ionica appointed administrators. The shares were suspended at 17.5p, having fallen under 9p a few days earlier. Investors have lost everything – yet anyone half-awake could have seen it coming and sold long before the end, before they lost the lot.

You can easily stop yourself losing your entire investment. If you make a simple rule to sell if ever you should lose, say, half of your money, you will be left with £500 out of any investment of £1,000. If you also decide (though I would not recommend it) to sell every time you double your money, you will have £2,000 for your £1,000.

Put the two investments together – your dud which has halved, and your winner which has doubled. Together, they have turned your £2,000 stake into £2,500. That is a 25% gain. Not wonderful, but not bad. Better than most unit trusts do most years. In the average share in the average market, you may not spot anything which has either doubled or halved. But in the penny share market, that could easily happen. And, once again, you can usually sell a share on the way down, and choose how much you lose on the ones you get wrong. Penny shares do halve overnight sometimes – but not that frequently.

Winning Odds

A London Business School survey watches the risks and returns from investing in smaller companies. In the early Nineties, it found that the probability of at least doubling your money was vastly greater than the probability of losing the lot in most years. Only 14 shares on average became worthless each year in the decade to 1986, while an average 120 doubled.

No guarantees, of course. The survey was not looking at penny shares alone. It just covered the ground where penny shares abound. Anyone looking merely at the good years in the mid-Eighties could see, however, that the number of companies going bust was very much smaller than 14 a year. And the proportion of companies doubling their worth – or much better – must have been higher. Even in the trickier market mood at the beginning of the Nineties, relatively few companies crashed and burned their shareholders to a total frazzle.

Anyone looking at the ups and downs in the Nineties would have found that remarkably few public companies actually went to the wall. The number whose share prices doubled or better would have been remarkably high in the great bull run from 1992 to mid-1998. Smaller companies actually underperformed between 1993 and 1998, and the London Business School boys decided that small companies did not necessarily perform better, but differently. Anyone who believes in business cycles will appreciate that a poor showing in the mid-Nineties improves the odds on a superior performance over the next decade.

None of this provides the perfect demonstration that penny shares are poised to become real investment winners as well as being the most attractive gambling stocks – but it comes pretty close to confirming what penny stock players know in their hearts. With penny shares, the chances of doubling your money are very much better than the chances of losing the lot. And, just maybe, this could be the game to play for the Millennium.

Ignorance is Bliss

Simply because they are not normally among the Boots and Marks & Spencers, penny shares can have another crucial advantage for the small investor – less is known about them. That can be a double-edged sword, and means that there could be nasty surprises in store. But there are thousands of highly-trained City-types poring over documents, dealing with bigger businesses, seeking to spot money-making opportunities, working for firms with billions of pounds invested in the latest high technology communications systems, buying and selling shares around the world.

These stock-watchers are in the business of trying to persuade big money investors – pension funds, insurance companies and such – to buy or sell shares through their firms, so that those firms can earn a profit or commission on them. Big investors are happiest in big companies. Their fund managers are generally judged by how closely the performance of the shares they buy and sell matches the competition. A fraction better than the average is heaven, a significant amount below for more than a year or two, and the fund manager could be out on his ear.

That system does not favour the brave. It means that the mediocre, safe in the middle of the pack, rarely get criticised. Such chaps generally stick to what they think they, and the other fund managers, know about. That is the big companies, where they can trade shares easily. So many people spend so much time analysing big companies that they rarely spring big surprises. Their profits usually fall within a few million pounds of what City back-room boys estimate, partly because the back-room boys are quite good at their jobs, and partly because it spoils a company's reputation and share price to come up with too many shocks, so they usually steer analysts in the right direction.

The system irons out share price moves, up or down. Penny shares, though, tend to be in companies too modest to attract big investors. Back-room boys often ignore them. The best back-room boys are in a high-cost business, where they need to persuade investors to trade in tens or preferably hundreds of thousands of pounds a time. You cannot do that in penny shares. They are not deemed worth the bother, and they get overlooked. Many stockbroking houses will not allow their analysts to follow the tiddlers, simply because they cannot generate enough interest from their big money clients, no matter how good the story. Some big names will not bother with anything whose market value is under £500m. Get into smaller capitalisation stocks – say £100m market value or less – and you really might be into uncharted territory.

Such companies are not completely overlooked, of course. In the investment world, someone always knows more than you do. There are small funds specialising in smaller companies, or bigger investors punting a few penny shares to add spice. Many City brokers study smaller companies to make money for themselves. And now the internet has vastly improved access to information.

Nonetheless, the very real chance that you might be able to buy a fast-moving share before it gets big enough for the heavy mob to notice adds to the fun and profit potential of the penny game. Once a company moves into the major league, or even the second rank, the price can shift even faster as the big buyers pile in. So if penny stocks sometimes mean a journey into the unknown, it can have advantages. Ignorance may be bliss for the penny punter – a wonderful buying opportunity, the chance to get in before the big money spots the action.

Closer to the Chairman's Heart

Penny shares, too, can benefit from being closer to the chairman's heart. In these days of corporate correctness, Cadbury Codes and so on, few big companies are still dominated by the families who built them. They have grown too large for a small group to retain major influence, and the corporate investors do not like it anyway. So big businesses are generally run by professional managers.

No matter what the theory or how diligent the practice, few professional company directors have quite the same commitment to success as owner-managers. Many times, the professionals are men who have already carved out their position in life, and are comfortable with what they have got. The directors of some of our biggest companies often have few shares between them. They are simply very superior employees, big cogs in the wheel. Ego may spur them on, but they lack the life-and-death devotion of the man who built the business from the bottom and is determined to keep building.

Smaller companies, the kind most frequently in the penny share class, are more closely identified with individuals. And individuals determined to make money often light upon penny share companies as suitable vehicles for their ambitions. They can buy bigger pieces of smaller companies for less money. They offer a more affordable way into the game for new go-getters. As these men build their fortune, they build profits for shareholders who ride with them. They know the value of penny share companies, and the need to make them appeal to investors large and small. Many of the most rewarding success stories start with this background.

Penny Share Problems

Outlining the advantages can make penny shares sound exciting, so good that it is tempting to wonder why small investors ever buy anything else. But there are disadvantages and dangers particular to playing penny shares. It is not all sunshine and clear blue skies. Like everything in the investment world, the penny share game is ruled by the classic law – the greater the reward, the greater the risk.

Make no mistake, penny shares normally come with companies which are smaller, weaker, or less established than the average quoted company. Probably the greatest proportion are in companies which have seen better days, have been in decline for some time, and could go on declining if nothing is done.

Whatever the reason for the decline, because of their smaller size or financial fragility, penny share companies are among the most vulnerable to any setback – in the economy as a whole, in the industry where they operate, or simply in their own operations. They do go bust more often than the average UK company. In the early Nineties, perhaps forty quoted companies a year disappeared, leaving investors without a penny.

Surprisingly, though, there were almost as many bigger businesses among the casualties. They were able to load themselves with silly borrowings and over-ambitious plans in a fashion denied the smaller players. Size was no guarantee of safety. Bigger companies simply crashed on a bigger scale.

When everything is romping onward and upward, it is easy to forget that the whole stock market climate changes dramatically in bad times. And if few penny companies actually get pushed under, many may suffer a substantial share price setback. Those which raced to new peaks on hopes of action in a bull market will plunge more swiftly than they rose if no new initiatives have been taken by the time the market turns. In the prolonged uncertainty which followed the Crash of October 1987, many friendless penny shares plummeted to a quarter of their previous peaks. They tumbled so fast that many unsuspecting investors suddenly woke up to discover that the floor had gone before they even noticed it was moving. And in the months that followed, prices fell still further.

As we move into a new century, however, there are some similarities. After a long, hard grind, interest returned to penny shares in the mid-Nineties. Many enjoyed a wonderful run as small investors regained their nerve, and the big boys started to look for greater value than that on offer in the inflated ratings of the top 100 or so. The good times did not last, however, and after a quiet spell, many prices began to be pushed down to bargain levels by 1998. That is the mood which creates opportunities. As interest returns, prices often move up relatively quickly as demand outstrips supply. When business looks tough, that is the time for the selective penny share punter to pounce, buying real value, looking towards the inevitable swing back into fashion. And in the year 2000, it is back with a vengence.

The Roller-Coaster Trap

Penny share prices can ride a roller-coaster, thrilling when they soar, sickening when they slump. The market in penny shares is less efficient than in bigger stocks. There are fewer people ready to buy and sell them. Whereas there could be a dozen places or more for your stockbroker to trade big-name shares, many penny shares may rely on only one market-maker to set the price. There could be times when he will not want to buy or sell, never mind about Stock Exchange rules. He has no competition to fear, no worries about anyone stealing his business. If he does not want to play, no-one is going to be able to force him to make a sensible price.

That accentuates price changes, up or down. And when shares are on the slide, the moves could be even sharper than on the rise. No-one, after all, wants to buy large quantities of a share which they may have to hold for ages because no-one else will buy, and which could continue to fall much lower. So prices get slammed, hard and fast.

While it is possible to deal in 250,000 shares in Sainsburys without anyone batting an eye lid, even in good times it may not be possible to trade in more than 5,000 shares of some penny stocks, perhaps much less. There may be fewer shares in existence to trade, of course, and a large slug of them may be held by directors or others reluctant to sell. In a rising market, that sends prices up more rapidly. But if someone comes on with a big selling order, it could send the price tumbling dramatically, for reasons which may have nothing to do with the health of the company or its prospects. Out of the blue, your bright and shiny penny share could suddenly look very tarnished. You will not know why, and might be unable to discover any reason. The setback could last for months, years even, if a big seller is dribbling out shares in a reluctant market.

Selling Snags

Worst of all, perhaps, is the danger that it could suddenly become difficult to sell more than small numbers – or, indeed, any at all – of many penny stocks in a downturn. Overnight, the dealing size could shrink to a mere 500 shares where it once was possible to buy or sell 5,000.

Getting locked into a falling share is a depressing, costly experience, and it taught many punters a nasty lesson in the great slump of 1974. By holding on for happier times, some may have got their money back – and eventually multiplied it ten, twenty or more times over. But if you needed your cash when the crunch was on, and could find no-one to buy at any price, it was almost worse than losing it altogether. The warning that you should only play the share market with money you can afford to lose is no ritual, empty chant. Many an investor learnt the weight of that lesson again after October 1987. There were signs that it was coming home to them yet again in some small stocks late in the summer of 1998.

If you can take a long view, of course, a slump may bring marvellous buying opportunities. The crash of 1973 and 1974 saw the average public company share price fall by about 75p in the pound. In January 1975, the *Financial Times* index was down to 146, less than one tenth of the levels twelve years later. Shares in some of our biggest name businesses, like Grand Metropolitan (now part of Diageo) and Forte (now tucked away in Granada), were down in the penny stock class. In the following ten or twelve years, many of them multiplied twenty or thirty fold in value, a real penny share treat.

The October 1987 Crash brought few such dramatic setbacks. Where it did, several companies eventually went bust, failing beneath the weight of absurdly heavy borrowing. Others, like advertising agents Saatchi & Saatchi, or leisure group Brent Walker, were left to struggle, survive and rebuild, with the interest of Ordinary Shareholders diluted by heavy new share issues and capital reconstructions. Brent Walker never made it back, though Saatchi & Saatchi eventually got it together again. Perhaps Saatchi's great advertising agency rival, WPP, provided the most remarkable example of how to rise and fall and rise again. Under Martin Sorrell, the man who led it into trouble, it was reconstructed to achieve great gains for investors in the Nineties.

Any market setback pushes some erstwhile big names down into the penny share class. Sometimes they make it back, but the best penny share opportunities may not be among the faded stars. Most of the big names which hit trouble tend either to go completely, or become so heavily handicapped by debt and extra burdens that it is a very long haul before they look really attractive. Perhaps the most interesting areas are among medium-sized companies which have shrunk, or the smaller ones which have become real tiddlers, but that have continued to trade, and are ready to give up and sell to someone new who wants to use the share listing to reshape the company. More of that later.

The Cost Crunch

Higher risks are one thing, but the biggest abiding practical problem with penny shares in good times or bad is the 'cost crunch'. The opportunity of playing the market with modest sums of money makes penny shares highly attractive, but the everyday, utterly routine and inescapable expense burden is a depressing disincentive.

The Dealing Spread

The share price you see in most newspapers or on TV, is not what you pay when you buy or get when you sell. It is the middle price. In the real market, shares are traded on a bid and offer basis. Bid is what you get for your shares when you sell, offered is what they are offered to you at – what you pay to get them. The most widely quoted price you see is arrived at by taking the middle of those prices. So a share listed in the press at 98p may actually be 96p if you want to sell, 100p to buy. If it is a popular share in a big company, the 98p middle price may actually mean 97p to sell, or 99p to buy. Or, perhaps, even 97.5p to sell and 98.5p if you want to buy.

The difference between the buying and selling price is the dealing spread. It can be a killer in penny shares. Crudely, the spread is the profit which goes to the market-maker, the wholesaler who handles the trade in different blocks of shares when your bank or broker deals for you.

The size of the spread is determined largely by demand and competition. Shares in major companies can be traded on a tiny spread, because they change hands in large numbers, and because there are several market-makers competing for the business. Penny shares are different. In practice, many will be handled by one market-maker. There may be two or three in theory, but often one market-maker dominates, and the others follow his prices, ready to trade only in tiny quantities.

That means the spread can be very wide, and is a hefty proportion of the price. Take, for example, a share with a middle price of 10p. The market-maker's quotation could be 9p bid (if he is buying), 11p offered (when he is selling), a spread of 2p, or 20% of the middle price.

Expensive? Of course. Think about it. If you buy, change your mind immediately, and decide to re-sell, what happens? You bought for 11p, sold for 9p, and you have lost 2p instantly on a share you thought cost 10p before you started. If you had intended to spend £500 on 5,000 shares, you actually had to put up £550. When you sold, you got only £450 back. In two quick moves, you have lost £100, and your original intended £500 investment has tumbled to £400. And that is before the commission you pay your stockbroker for doing this dumb deal. Bad news.

Never mind. It could easily have been worse. Say the market-maker had guessed your broker was a seller when the broker contacted him to execute your sale. The market-maker could easily have altered his price to his own advantage, and called the shares 8p to 10p, so you would have lost another £25.

Even if you plan to stay with your new penny share, you could find your nerve is tested if you watch the price closely. Because the price is small, each change will be made in greater proportional steps than with higher-priced shares. The popular stock I mentioned earlier, perhaps trading at 97.5p to 98.5p, may shift in units of .5p a time. So if the next change was down, it would be called 97p to 98p, a middle price of 97.5p. Nothing to worry about. Anyone who bought at 98.5p, would get only 97p back if they sold now. And a loss of 1.5p in the pound is hardly significant.

But with penny shares, mere halfpenny moves slash a hole in the sums. If the price falls in units of .5p, it means that the first change from the middle price of 10p will take it to 9.5p. On a middle price of 9.5p, the market-maker's quotation will be 8.5p if he buys, 10.5p if he sells. Anyone who bought with the 10p middle price in mind will suddenly find that the 5,000 shares they paid 11p for – or £550 before expenses – could be sold for 8.5p each, or £425. In one move, £125 has gone.

And so it goes on, and on, and on. The dealing spread can be devastating. A fall from 10p to 8p may look like an uncomfortable 20% drop on paper, but in hard cash, it is much worse. It would mean that an investment of £550 is suddenly down to £350 – before expenses which could easily take a loss of £200 up to £250, or half of the £500 our punter had in mind when the newspapers quoted the share at 10p. Calamity.

The spread problem looks less damaging when a share is rising, of course. Once you are ahead, it makes the fun come faster. Every .5p rise on a penny share is worth more than a .5p rise in a heavyweight.

Even so, the dealing spread does delay your break-even point, and stacks the odds against you. That 10p middle price may look good when the shares are quoted up 2p to 12p in the newspaper. The 20% profit may sound nice. In fact, it will be an illusion. The 12p middle may mean a market-maker's price of

11p bid, 13p offered. Since the 10p share actually cost you 11p, you are breaking even WITHOUT counting expenses like broking commission. The expenses mean you need another move up, to a middle price of 12.5p before you have covered your buying costs. And don't forget the second batch of dealing costs when you sell.

Suddenly, the penny game looks tougher. It has taken a 25% rise in the price just to come out even. You begin to understand why many people stick to the popular, bigger companies with heavier prices. If you had bought that big company share at 98.5p, you would have been breaking even, after expenses, at about 108p, a rise of about 9%. Much easier.

Think about it carefully, but do not despair. A good penny share will shrug these killer costs off easily. When it moves, if it moves the right way, it should go much further, much faster than the big boys. But the routine price of playing in penny shares is steeper than it seems at first glance. Be sure you understand that – and there are more costs to come.

Trading Costs

That 25% gain in our example would cover the costs of trading, as well as the dealing spread – but only just. Trading costs are the other irritating burden of the penny share game. Nowadays, many brokers will not accept orders without making a minimum charge of £20. Outside London, there are some who will. Treasure them.

A minimum £20 charge bears more heavily on an investment of £500 than on one of £1,000, especially since you will have to pay it both when you buy and again when you sell. You may have to pay value added tax at 17.5% on the broker's commission, though some incorporate it in their minimum charge. You are also charged stamp duty of .5% of the value of your deal when you buy. That adds £2.50 on each £500 trade. If you do really well, and hit the big time, there is a 60p levy on each deal over £5,000.

There has been a great fuss about trading charges, with leading brokers withdrawing low-cost dealing schemes, claiming that their back offices simply have not been able to cope with the flood of paperwork. So the cost of dealing, which weighs more heavily on penny share players than most, is likely to continue to rise. More bad news, unless the advent of internet share trading can come to the rescue of private investors.

Net and telephone trading is happening, but is not without problems and dangers. Some execution-only dealers offer a poor service. Many investors have experienced long delays in getting through on the phone, and have lost money as their shares moved while they waited. The ability to execute deals on-line, over the internet, is fine while it works, and does cut costs. Once again, though, there are interruptions to services, delays in getting through. If the market should fall sharply, you can bet brokers offering phone services of one sort or another will be flooded, and the system may well break down. So be careful about signing up to save a few pounds. If you can get one (and it is difficult), an account where you can talk to a real live broker is worth the extra cost.

Clearly there are good reasons for being nervous about playing penny shares. The burdens listed above are not the only ones you will have to bear. Add the some-time threat that management and accounting standards are not always what they ought to be in smaller companies, and the unfortunate fact that they do suffer an occasional dose of down-right dishonesty, and you have a cocktail which some might consider altogether too lethal.

Go in with your eyes wide open, however, and there is no reason not to play. Penny shares are fun, and can make you big money. Pick a sensible penny punt, and the pluses far outweigh the minuses. In the rest of this book, I hope I can help you duck the penny dreadfuls, and fasten on to a few of the flyers.

TWO

Are You Fit for the Penny Share Game?

✷

The penny share game CAN make you a fortune. Really. Dream a while. If you had put just £5,000 into the Ordinary shares of First National Finance Corporation near their bottom in 1975, you would have made your £1m comfortably by 1986. If you had picked Polly Peck around their nadir of 9p in the late Seventies, and put just £2,500 in, it would have taken you three years to become a millionaire when it hit £36. If you bought Durlacher at 4p in 1998, just £1,000 would have been worth £1m in 1999.

Pick your own examples. Weave your own dreams. It does not take too much effort to imagine such fantastic killing. There are shares – penny shares, all of them – which score almost unbelievable gains.

It may be that no-one outside the companies actually managed to make the millionaire club on the strength of First National Finance, Polly Peck or Durlacher. Certainly, I have never come across anyone who did. But a lot of people did make a lot of money, and turned a few thousand pounds into hundreds of thousands of pounds. No matter how improbable it seems, new shooting stars do appear every so often. In the Eighties, Pentland Industries rocketed from the equivalent of 20p to more than 3,000p, allowing for capital changes. Just think – a £2,000 investment would have been worth over £300,000. It is like winning the National Lottery or the football pools – only better. You do not lose the whole of your stake each week if you do not win.

Those are the dreams. They can come true. Even in the recession-wracked early Nineties, several penny shares doubled or trebled. One Monday morning, early in 1992, I tipped P.E. Kemp in the *Daily Mail* at 4p. Three days later, it was suspended at 7p pending a big acquisition. In the spring of 1993, I tipped

Millwall in the *Daily Mail* at 2.5p. A couple of months later, it touched 6.5p. You could easily have dealt in 250,000, buying and selling. I know one investor who traded in and out of four million of them. Seven years later, Millwall is back around 1p, and still attracting penny share punters. The winners are around, all of the time, but you always need to remember – shares are for selling as well as buying.

In the last year or two, some of the winnings have been almost obscene. City slickers have been making fortunes. They always do. But everywhere I go, I meet people who have made hundreds of thousands, maybe millions, playing the market. They are not just the insiders. Many are private punters, people who started with tens of thousands and have gambled, often picking soar-away penny shares.

In April 1999, I started my own website www.michaelwalters.com to help people keep in closer touch with my tips. In the spring of 2000, it has tens of thousands of regular visitors. Many have sent me e-mails thanking me for tips which have helped them take a few thousand pounds and make it into tens of thousands. Others tell me of the winners they have spotted. However they have done it, I am delighted. Often those winnings have been made in penny shares.

There are people who tell me they have been able to save their businesses, take holidays, organise special trips with grand-children to the theatre in London, buy new equipment for the kitchen, and simply have fun trading in shares. Many have not made really big money, but just enough to make a difference.

For most penny share punters, giant gains will remain distant dreams. Most punters will not make a massive killing. Many will be delighted to double or treble their money. Others will end up grateful for any profit at all. Some will lose, blowing all of their investment, or a hefty part of it. But everyone should have fun doing it, knowing that by playing the penny share game, they have at least given themselves the chance of making the dream come true, no matter how remote the odds of landing the really big one.

Time and again, it is important to return to reality, to emphasise that playing penny shares is a risky business, with no guarantee of success. It could mean you lose all of your investment.

Understand that, please. And examine your motives and your nerve quite carefully. You may not be fit for the penny share game. It may be best for you to stay away.

No-one should consider entering the stock market with money they cannot afford to lose. If you are going to buy shares of any sort, from the biggest and best-respected public companies to the smallest, scattiest speculation, you are taking a risk. The Government insists that advertisements for unit trusts carry a warning that share prices can fall as well as rise. So they should. Buying any sort of share can damage your wealth. Stock Exchange investment is dangerous.

Every share punter knew about Brent Walker, for example, in the Eighties. Some believed detailed circulars from the company's brokers saying it had assets of £10 a share. Some bought the shares for over 400p. By the late Nineties, it has been long gone. Other big names like British & Commonwealth, Polly Peck and Maxwell Communication have joined it. So has Trafalgar House, which owned the Ritz and the Cunard shipping line.

Other famous names live on, but are among the walking wounded. The once magical name of Laura Ashley barely limps along, British Biotech, once cheer leader for a whole exciting industry, is struggling, House of Fraser has upset investors galore, Rank Group has been forced to fire its chief executive as profits wilt. Question marks are rising over some of the biggest names in Britain, and their share prices have fallen sharply. No-one is safe. No share can ever guarantee to generate a profit for investors. And when the economic cycle slips from boom towards slump, the dangers grow greater for everyone.

There are thousands of shares to choose from. Very few will turn out to be worthless. But at any time, the price of almost any of them, in companies large or small, could fall, and fall quite sharply. What happens if you need the cash at that point? If the car goes crunch, the roof starts leaking, and the TV goes on the blink, all at once? And you have put all of your savings, not into a risky penny share, but into the estimable Lloyds TSB?

You can sell your shares in Lloyds TSB, of course. It could take a couple of weeks before you get your money. That could be a problem. But what about the market? What if you bought Lloyds TSB for £10, and the price is £6? After your buying and selling costs, the £1,000 you put in has shrunk to less than £600 by the time you get your cheque. You are in trouble.

It was easy to suffer that sort of loss in, say, 1998, if you got your timing wrong. Any number of sound, solid, trust-worthy investments could have brought losses of 25% of more in a good year – if you needed the money back at the wrong moment.

And 1998 was not a bad year for the market. Go back to 1973 and 1974, when a great stock market boom suddenly whip-lashed into slump. Or October 1987, when the *Financial Times* index lost 500 points in two days, and the average share lost a quarter of its value. Each time, careers were ruined, lives shattered, marriages broken. Countless share punters who had begun to think the golden gains would never end, who had bought that villa in Spain, a yacht, or even just a new car, suddenly found they were trapped in a falling market.

While the *Financial Times* index may have dropped from 600 to 146 in 1974, many, many shares plunged far more dramatically. The National Westminster Bank issued a statement to try to reassure the City that all was well, Burmah Oil had to be bailed out by the Bank of England, property companies toppled. Shares galore slumped – not just by the market average of three-quarters, down from 100p to 25p, but from 150p or more to 20p or less. If you were able to hold on into the late Seventies, or to the Eighties and Nineties, you would have made most of your losses back, and more. But if you needed to sell in the mid-Seventies, you could have been wiped out.

The October 1987 Crash was followed by a partial recovery, and by September 1991, the index was pushing to a new record. It made new peaks in 1993. But some big name companies, especially in the property sector, were down from over 200p to under 20p – or were bust. The house market, apparently unstoppable in 1987, had established three dismal years of sharply falling prices. Jobless totals were rising, and industry all across the country was struggling. A nervous market hovered, trying to decide whether it was at the bottom of a slump, ready for recovery, or poised for another setback. Anyone who picked the wrong share in the Eighties could still have been regretting it in the mid-Nineties.

Ancient history? Perhaps. But history has a habit of repeating itself. Remember the Great Slump of 1929, and the Wall Street Crash, with legends of bodies flying from windows? And you may recall sitting in school, hearing about the South Sea Bubble, a share crash which changed the course of British history in 1720. There were slumps a plenty over the next 200 years. There will be more over the next 200 – perhaps starting when you least expect them. That is how it usually goes. Once the great mass of investors becomes convinced that the market can only go up, it turns around and zaps them.

You do not even need a market slump, or a slippery share price to hit trouble either. Suppose you had joined the great legion of Sids, and bought shares in British Gas when the Government privatised it in the autumn of 1986. A sensible move. British Gas shares showed a tasty profit from the moment trading began, and hardly faltered for ages. But what if you had needed your cash in a hurry? Irritated by your bank, unable to find a stockbroker, you went to one of the dealers advertising in some sections of the financial press (not the *Daily Mail*, it should be noted. The *Mail* tries very hard to vet financial advertising). They sounded fast and efficient over the phone, you got a reasonable price, and sent your share certificate. Then the cheque did not come back on time, and next thing you knew, the business had closed, and you were standing in a long line of creditors, hoping the receiver would be able eventually to recover a few pence in the pound for you. The share was right, the company you thought was a respectable stockbroker was wrong.

That sort of scam should have been banished by now, thanks to a forest full of new regulations. No-one will get caught quite that way again. But there is a new confidence trickster in the wings every month, with a different way of parting naive punters from their money. It would be wrong to make too much of this sort of danger. Most people you deal with will be perfectly honest. Most investors will never experience any problems. But always be on your guard. You never quite know.

Get through this book, and you will not be so foolish as to trade with the wrong people. Thousands have done so, through the Seventies, Eighties and Nineties. It can be dangerous out there. Share investment can bring calamity if you are not properly prepared.

Do not think it cannot happen to you. It probably will not. But the only sensible way to have fun and profit in the share market is to use nothing but cash you can afford to lose.

Be sure of one thing – unless you are very lucky, or too timid to trade more than a couple of times, you will end up losing money on some deals, no matter how carefully you vet them, or how good they look.

The Financial Essentials

Emphasising the dangers does distort overall impressions, however. Look beyond the ups and downs, and you will see that the stock market rises steadily over the longer term. In the end, it offers a good hedge against inflation. But because of the short-term swings, if you want to play, you must sort out your financial essentials first. Look to the roof over your head. Make sure you have enough to pay the rent or cover your mortgage payments each month. If you are married, take out a mortgage protection policy to be sure that, if anything happens to you, the mortgage is paid off on your death. Take out a sensible amount of life insurance to help your family survive without you. Three or four times annual salary is reasonable.

It is important, too, to buy permanent health insurance, to guarantee income for a while if you should be unable to work. Check that you have a proper pension from your employer. Make additional voluntary contributions as early as you can afford to. Take out a personal pension if in doubt.

Then there is the nest-egg. Leave it safe, untouched, untempted by the stock market. Slap it into the National Savings Investment Bank (especially good if you pay little or no tax because it pays out the interest without taking tax off first), or a building society. Interest rates at the banks are generally less attractive. Whatever you do, play it safe. Keep a chunk of cash where you are sure it will always be available and easy to withdraw. Do not be tempted by higher-than-average interest rates. That almost certainly means higher-than-average risks. You will be taking risks enough with your money in the stock market.

Unit Trusts

Life support systems in place, you ought then to think about dipping a toe into the share market by buying a unit trust, or an investment trust, or starting a Personal Equity Plan. There are over 1,400 unit trusts, so picking the right one is a problem. Use a good independent investment adviser, or stick to the biggest names, and buy off-the-page through newspaper advertisements.

Check first how much money the company manages. As a crude safety test, only go for established names managing over £1,000 million of funds. There are lots. Among those I like are M&G, Save & Prosper, Perpetual, GT, Mercury, the Prudential, and Fidelity. Pick their general trusts, or the international trusts. For a dash of spice, try the special situations trusts.

Do not go for exotic specialist funds, those which invest in one industry, emerging markets, or one distant land. They may prosper awhile, but are more volatile. Those who plumped for Far Eastern funds or the odd investment in Russia have suffered heavy losses in the late Nineties. Ideally, you ought to choose something solid and steady. If you do go direct, ask the managers for a discount, especially if you are spending over £2,000. You might not get it, but some will play ball, especially if you intend a large investment. Check, too, that the managers have a cash fund you can switch into cheaply if you get worried that the market is in for a long decline. That makes sense.

Unit trusts try to take the fiddle and much of the risk out of investing by employing an expert manager to choose shares on behalf of unit-holders. The trust will buy perhaps between 40 and 120 shares with the aim of making money in the area outlined by the trust's objectives. There are trusts specialising in almost anything, from obscure American companies, to high technology stocks, gold shares, and the big names in the High Street.

In recent years, there has been a vogue for 'Tracker' funds. These heavily publicised trusts invest their money in shares of the leading 100 or so companies, the ones whose prices are used to determine the FT-SE 100 share index. That index is the main measure of overall stock market performance. Over the medium term, it tends to advance. It is used as the main yard-stick against which funds measure their own progress.

Active managers seek to beat the index, but often fail. Tracker funds are supposed to duplicate the performance of the index (to track it). Because the market rises over the medium to long term, Trackers are marketed as the ideal way to take a low-risk exposure to leading shares. That is sound enough. The trouble is that when the economic cycle turns down and shares begin to fall, the Tracker fund will also fall in value by roughly the same proportion. The manager of an active unit trust, picking different shares, should avoid some of that fall – in theory, at least.

So anyone going for a Tracker must take a long-term view, and be prepared to accept setbacks. Or, perhaps, to sell the Tracker or switch to a cash fund, when it appears times are getting tough. That, though, defeats the object of paying a professional to make the difficult investment decisions for you. On the whole, Trackers are useful and sensible for those who want some relatively safe, long-term market exposure. And they should bear lower management costs than other funds.

With a Tracker or any unit trust, each unit-holder effectively owns a tiny fraction of each share the trust holds. As the price of those shares moves up or down, so does the value of the units. The manager sends regular reports to unit holders, and there should be a ready market in the units, allowing you to get your money out quickly. Because the trust invests in a wide spread of shares, and is run in accordance with strict rules imposed by the Department of Trade, it should offer a good degree of security. Unit trusts do not go bust, though if you pick a specialist that falls out of favour, you could see your investment fall sharply in value. No manager, no matter how good, will be able to make money in a falling market.

In general, unit trusts are excellent for new investors who do not want to do it themselves. They are also more attractive than a building society for long-term savings, apart from vital, rock-solid rainy day cash. Unit trust values rise and fall with the share market, but, over an extended period, the returns should beat a building society hands-down.

Building societies can generally only offer fixed-interest investments, with a return which is constantly under attack from inflation, though most societies will help you buy unit trusts. Unit trusts should offer a reasonable income, which can generally be re-invested automatically, plus capital growth which will outpace inflation comfortably. Once again, though, there are no guarantees.

Investment Trusts

Investment trusts are broadly similar to unit trusts. They employ managers to pick shares and buy them on behalf of the trusts, searching for capital growth or high income. But investment trusts have a set capital. They issue a fixed number of shares to raise a certain amount, and that is it. They can come to the market for more, but that is comparatively rare. So when you buy into an investment trust, you buy the shares of that trust. They are traded on the stock market like any other share, and the price responds to supply and demand. That supply and demand is influenced in turn by how well the fund is performing. If the manager has picked lots of winners, and the value of the trust's holdings is going up, demand for the shares will rise, and the price of the shares should go up. And vice versa.

In practice, it has been the custom for most investment trust shares to sell at prices beneath the value of the shares they own – a discount. In bad times, that discount can be as high as 35%. More recently, it has been 10% or less. It means that when you buy an investment trust share, you tend to get more assets for your money than you do with a unit trust.

This can be a useful advantage, but discounts can rise as well as fall, and so investment trust price movements are not always straightforward. Trusts do sometimes receive a takeover bid, usually at asset value, so the price will rise to eliminate the discount. That is a potential advantage not open to a unit trust (unit trusts trade on asset value). In the past, management charges have been low for investment trusts, but as they have become more popular and more widely marketed in the Nineties, costs have risen.

From time to time, some trust shares actually trade at a premium to asset value. By and large, it is not a good idea to buy when that happens.

A good investment trust, however, can be better than a unit trust. The practical differences now are not great in the case of the best trusts. Pick whichever takes your fancy, unit trusts or investment trusts. Both offer a relatively safe way of getting into the market with the benefit of experienced management.

Individual Savings Accounts

There are two ways of getting into unit trusts or investment trusts – either by buying them directly, or by taking out an Individual Savings Account (ISA) which puts cash into unit or investment trust shares. For most would-be investors, an ISA is a sensible first direct venture into shares, and depending on the amount of cash you have, should be the home for the first few thousand pounds of your risk money.

As from 5 April, 2000, the rules allow you to put £5,000 a year into an ISA. The details are unnecessarily complicated, and you can have maxi-ISAs, mini-ISAs, and split your investment in all sorts of ways.

You really ought to consult an Independent Financial Adviser about the details. Some of them offer discounts on the commission, so they do deliver value for your money. There are many perfectly sound and respectable IFAs. My favourite for many years has been Hargreaves Lansdown in Bristol. They may not be perfect – who is ? — but on the whole they are sensible people with a well thought-out approach to these things. Their phone number is 01179 767 767. They also have a website, www.HargreavesLansdown.co.uk. It may also be worth checking internet sites like Moneyworld at www.moneyworld.co.uk and Interactive Investor International on www.iii.co.uk/isa.

Fairly simply, an ISA allows you a tax-free wrapper to put around £5,000 of savings each year. You escape capital gains tax on the investments in the ISA, and until 2004 can get a 10% tax credit for dividends from qualifying shares in UK companies. The investment can be split in a variety of ways. Some can go into cash or insurance funds, or it can go into an investment trust or a unit trust, which makes a sensible first step towards owning shares.

It is also possible to choose shares yourself as a way of using the £5,000 stake in a self-select ISA. Unfortunately, only shares quoted on a recognised stock exchange qualify. That can be pretty daft, since it does not allow you to buy shares on the Alternative Investment Market, while you can put in shares traded on many overseas markets. You cannot include shares traded on Ofex, the more lightly regulated trading facility operated by J.P. Jenkins outside the Stock Exchange. Since that is effectively a nursery for smaller, more speculative companies, that will not trouble you in the early stages of any investment adventure, since you should not be putting your money there.

You cannot simply buy shares yourself, and tell the taxman they are part of your ISA. Given the state's determination to meddle in all we do, you have to set up an ISA through some sort of investment management firm. Many of them offer an ISA where they will select the shares for you. Others – often stockbrokers – will allow you to set up an ISA where you select the shares. They will charge you for this privilege, of course.

If you are using an ISA for a relatively secure chunk of your savings, and want one managed by someone else, go for the big names. They may be boring, and may not do particularly well, but they will not run off with your money, and there are all sorts of people you can complain to if they do something wrong. Complaining does not do you much good – the regulators really exist to make rules, not to help you – but the fact that there is a regulator stops the worst excesses.

There will be exciting returns advertised by some fund groups. Do not take too much notice. In this business, what does well in one year rarely does so well for long. Top of the performance charts is often bottom a year or two later. So the bland, middle of the road boys are best. If you are going to gamble in penny shares yourself, you want your ISA cash as a sort of first reserve. Above all, you want it safe. So settle for the big boring average fund in a well-known name. That way there may not be particularly good performance, but there should be no really nasty surprises.

Tempting though it may seem, do not go to smaller firms, newer companies, or local managers. They might outperform the monsters, but in this instance, you want something solid and secure. And though I love them, newer more aggressive managers do tend to come unstuck more often. Sorry.

What Makes a Penny Share Punter

Only when you have made proper financial provisions and know you have money which you can afford to take a little less seriously – can afford to lose – should you even think about penny shares.

There are no rules to say that investors cannot take the penny share market seriously. Goodness knows, there is very serious money to be made in penny shares. The pickings can be rich enough to attract the biggest investment houses from time to time. Nonetheless, the notion persists in the traditional reaches of the City that penny shares are somehow something for the spivvier end of the market, not worthy of the in-depth analytical overkill which attends our bigger companies. And the people who play around in them are considered not quite what they should be.

It is nonsense, of course, a hangover from the days when the City was much more worried about the class system, before the meritocracy clambered aboard, and long before the Big Bang made money, money, and yet more money the absolute king. The 'them and us' image of the City clings on here and there, though it is being swept aside, not least by public dismay at the disgraceful behaviour of some company fat cats and the insiders in the Lloyd's insurance market, in the Guinness affair, and at one or two blue-blooded merchant banks and stockbrokers. So do not allow anyone to tell you what to think about investment. Do it your way.

However, no matter how carefully you have arranged your financial affairs, and however well-prepared you are to lose the money you have ear-marked for penny shares, you need to recognise that getting your financial affairs in good order is not sufficient qualification alone for becoming a penny share punter. It needs a certain mental attitude. You need to be a gambler.

Be honest with yourself. You are in it for the money – and for a bit of fun. You may not gamble on the horses, or approve of throwing your cash around in a casino – but you are as much a punter as the boys who scour the racing pages each day.

It is nothing to be ashamed of unless it worries you yourself. Whatever the authorities may try to say, and whatever function it serves in raising money for British industry, the stock market is little more than a highly sophisticated casino with two different classes of player – those who admit they are gambling, and those who are fooling themselves.

It is important that anyone playing the penny share market recognises just what they are doing, why they are there. Anything else is a recipe for disaster. There is no point pretending you are laying down your money for the national good, or in thinking it may be rash and irresponsible to leap in and out of shares at great speed. If you want to become involved in the debate about whether investors take too short-term a view for the health of British industry, forget it. Leave that to the blimps. You will be taking investment too seriously. You will be in grave danger of becoming too inflexible, or losing sight of why you bought shares – to make money for yourself. Rest assured, the other penny share players will be playing by that rule – self-interest above all.

The Right Temperament

You must be made of the right stuff for the penny share game. If you do not have the temperament to gamble, forget it. If you lie awake wondering whether you will lose your stake, worrying about the next move in the price of your shares, give it up. It is not worth it for you. Sleepless nights do not make stock market winners.

Investing should be fun. It certainly can be. There are few absolutes in our lives. But doubling or trebling your money in a share is an absolute winner. There is no arguing, no 'ifs' and 'buts' when you have pocketed a big profit. You have done it. You got it right. The feeling of elation in a winning deal can be enormous, almost satisfaction enough in itself, without the money.

Get it wrong, though, and a sickening churning hits the pit of your stomach. There is no ducking it. The money is gone, and there is no retrieving it. It would be foolish to pretend that there is a way of rationalising losses away, of convincing yourself that you always knew it could happen and you were ready for it. When it happens – and if you do not come a cropper at some stage you will be a very lucky punter indeed – it hurts. You have to be ready to take it, and move on to the next situation – but not too quickly.

Share gambling can be a bug. It can take over and dominate your life. I have seen friends and work-mates lose their homes through stupid share trading. And go on to lose still more, and to damage their health. I have known wealthy City characters kill or cripple themselves through share dealings. It does happen. Believe me, this is no routine warning, one to be shrugged off. Stop. Think about it. There may be a flippant air at times about this book, and there is certainly much to encourage people to try their hand at the penny share game. But it can go wrong – badly wrong. Do not let it happen to you.

Patience and Persistence

Be prepared, too, to be patient and persistent. There is one classic shell company I have stumbled across from time to time for twenty years (I will not tell you the name. Who knows? It might be roaring away today). I do not understand why it has never been taken up and taken off. I watched another for twelve years until someone moved in to try to inject new life. It ran nicely for a while, quadrupled, and fluttered back. It was not until two or three years later that a second new team moved in, and started to reshape it yet again. Now, at last, it is flying.

Timing can be one of the most elusive investment qualities, yet one of the most crucial. So often, plans take longer to develop than expected. Sometimes it is necessary to be very patient, holding a promising share for ages before it begins to move. Often, discovering just what is going on, what might happen, takes great persistence, looking through company documents, perhaps checking at Companies House, trying to find a broker who knows what is afoot, reading the trade press for industry background. Remember – there is always someone who knows more about what is going on than you do.

Insider Trading

No matter how tough the Government tries to make the rules, how hard the fall of Ivan Boesky and the attendant host of American insiders, and what triumphs international co-operation may score in the battle against big-time cheats, insider trading will always be with us. It helps make the market go round.

The flow of information is essential to the share market. Some may buy and sell on instinct alone (don't knock it), and others may go in near-blind, trusting to luck. But the boys who move markets trade on what they know, gleaned from who they know. They deal because they think they know something the rest of us do not, or have not interpreted correctly.

It is hard to see, sometimes, what distinguishes inside information – important, illegal, unfair and unavailable to other investors – from a shrewd understanding of items which others may have overlooked, helped perhaps by a quiet word from somebody in the company who can confirm what it really means. Where does detailed research, following every move a company makes by talking to anyone who will talk, spill over into unacceptable intrusion? Which figures let out by a salesman over a friendly pint in the pub go just a shade too far? How can you distinguish between the stockbroker who recognises a car number plate outside a rival company's office and guesses at a merger, and the stockbroker who takes a personal call from someone in the company and is told which chairman was called in for very private talks?

It is impossible to stamp out insider trading completely. Greed will always be with us. If you object to operating in a system with insider trading at the core, shun shares. Play the game long enough, and you will find you are chasing insider information yourself, even if you are simply cross-examining the chairman over a glass of sherry at the annual meeting.

Recognise that intelligent anticipation of new information is a powerful factor in shifting share prices. You cannot fight it. Learn to read how it works, and use that knowledge to your advantage. It may not always be obvious, but share prices are influenced by what the other chap knows, even if no-one ever notices it, and even if that inside information is used simply to encourage someone to hold on, effectively stopping shares going up or down.

You may never discover why some price changes happen out of the blue. Never get too confident about how you can assess any situation. Share prices can dump you flat on your face, catching you out when you least expect it. Arrogance is not a quality which makes money for the small investor. You never learn enough, you can never afford to stop asking questions, watching for clues. If you think you can win at the penny share game because you got your first few moves right, you are heading for a fall. There is absolutely no substitute for inside information, or sheer good luck. But do not let it fool you. Luck does not last forever. And you are unlikely to get real inside information. That is usually confined to so-called professionals – the bankers, brokers, legal hangers-on who are involved in preparing deals. They usually get away with it, should they use it to cheat. The small fish – ones like you – get caught and fried.

It may seem strange, devoting a long section in a share book to the intangible business of the way you feel. It is vital, though, to successful investment. You will decide what to buy, what to sell, and when to do it, all on your own. There are no clear indicators, no absolute rules about how it is done. Never mind that some people suggest that the whole business may be locked into marvellous mathematical equations, with textbooks examining rows of figures and how they relate. Never mind that many in the fast-growing traded options market swear by a complex set of tables which determines whether prices are cheap or dear – in theory – and buy and sell by those rules. One of the chaps who devised those tables came a mighty cropper in the autumn of 1998. He was a director of a so-called hedge fund which required a £4bn bail-out. Suddenly, it seemed, the formulae did not quite come out right.

No-one gets it right every time. In the end, what makes prices move are the intangible emotions of investors. So pay attention to your own emotions. Ponder them. You may just decide that you are temperamentally unsuited for the penny share market and all that goes with it.

How Much Do You Need?

If you do want to play, it need not take much money. There are those who enjoy putting £50 or £100 into the share of their fancy. When they go up, they are overjoyed, though they are scarcely making money. Dealing costs make it impractical to play with such tiny amounts if profit is your aim. Perhaps £500 is a reasonable minimum, though there are no set rules.

Talk of constructing a portfolio is meaningless. There is no point trying to achieve any sort of balance – between growth and income, big companies and small, mature industries and new ventures, UK earners or export giants. Penny shares are about capital growth, without a care for income and dividends. If you get dividends as well, so much the better.

It would be foolish to put too much into any one share, foolish to spread your cash over too many shares. Too much in one, and you could have problems selling. Too many shares, and you may find it difficult to concentrate on what is happening in each of them. And though the impact of any loser will be reduced by the spread of your holdings, the impact of the winners will also be reduced by the non-movers. It is tough enough to find one flyer, let alone a dozen. So concentrate your efforts, but not too much. Five at a time ought to be plenty for the average penny share punter – though you make your own rules.

If you want to buy blind, pick 'em with a pin, and trust to luck – go to it. Sometimes it comes off. But if it does, just remember it is luck, not your special genius, and you should tuck some of your winnings away for a rainy day. You are unlikely to do it again, and only too likely to chance too much and blow the lot next time around.

THREE

What is a Penny Share?

✷

So far, we have been selling the sizzle and forgetting the steak, outlining the opportunities in penny shares without troubling to get down to hard and fast definitions.

It hardly matters. Everyone knows what a penny share is in practice – a share which does not cost too much, at a price which allows you to buy enough to make you feel you have got full weight for your money. Within reason, no-one worries too much about the boundary line – though they go too far in America. One store-keeper there once told me how he had done well with one of our British penny stocks – Jaguar. He had paid about 250p for it – a lot of pennies.

In the days before decimalisation, it was clear enough. There were twelve pennies in a shilling, twenty shillings in a pound. Penny shares were what the name suggested – shares which sold for pennies. Now, though, with 100 pence in a pound, definition is trickier. There are no hard and fast rules. A penny share is what you make it. Some suggest anything under 35p qualifies. Others go up to 50p. Yet others stretch it to 70p. But you know what inflation is. These days, we may be able to settle for anything up to 100p.

What really matters is the impression of quantity when you pick a penny share. Quality is an altogether different matter. Establishing that takes up a great deal of this book. But penny share investors like to feel they are getting more for their money. Psychologically, it seems much better to buy 5,000 shares for 10p each with your £500 than to buy just 500 shares for £1 apiece, or even 50 for £10 each. Yet there need be no difference at all in the fundamental worth of any of those shares, or even in the overall value of the underlying company.

If the company whose shares cost 10p has 50 million of them in issue, the whole company is valued at £5 million by the market. It could just as easily have 5 million shares in issue, trading at £1 each. The company would still be valued at £5m. Or the same company could have just 500,000 shares trading at £10 each – it would still be valued by the market at £5m.

Do Not be Fooled by the Price

So, the share you buy for 5p could easily be better value than the share you buy for 125p. Or much worse value. It depends on whether you are buying shares in a good company or a bad one – or whether the stock market thinks the company is good or bad. The basis for the price just goes back to a piece of accounting called 'par values'.

Par Values

By law in the United Kingdom, all shares must have a nominal, or par, value. Par value can be almost anything, but is usually between 1p and £1. A share with 1p nominal (or par) value is not necessarily worth 1p, any more than a £1 nominal value share is necessarily worth £1. A share is worth as much as someone will pay for it. Do not worry if you are buying a share with a 5p nominal value for 120p, or think you have a bargain by buying it for 2p. Nobody is ever going to give you 5p for that share just because that happens to be the nominal value.

Par, or nominal, values are most relevant when it comes to working out the actual amount of the dividend the company pays. Companies pay dividends to shareholders from the profits they make. Each share simply represents a small piece of the company. If you have one share in a company which has ten shares in issue, you own one-tenth of that company. The company will divide out the profits it makes by paying dividends to all shareholders. If you have one-tenth of the shares, you will get one-tenth of the profits which the directors decide should be distributed as dividends.

In public companies, of course, there are usually millions of shares in issue. So when you buy your 5,000 shares, you own only a very tiny fraction of the whole company. When it comes to working out dividends, they are announced as either so much per share, or so much per cent. A dividend of 2p a share is simple to understand. But a dividend of 20% is expressed as a proportion of the nominal value of that share, NOT the price of the share. So a 20% dividend on a 10p nominal share would be equivalent to a dividend of 2p a share. Or a 20% dividend on a £1 nominal share would be an actual payment of 20p for each share.

Splits and Scrips

Companies can change the nominal value of their shares. Sometimes they do it for special accounting reasons. Sometimes they do it just to shift into or out of the penny share category. By and large, private investors prefer shares with lighter prices. Even the biggest investors do not care overmuch for shares which are too far up in the heavyweight class, selling at £10 a time or more.

There is a powerful element of fashion and fancy in investment. Letting your share price soar too high and heavy simply puts people off, and may tend to prevent it from rising as far as it might. Many investors do not want to know about spending £3 or £4 on a single share. So company chairmen are keen to keep in favour, knowing that the more potential buyers there are for their stock, the better the price will perform.

There are two ways of keeping share prices slim: the share split, and the scrip, or capitalisation, issue. The split involves taking the nominal value, splitting it, and giving out an appropriate number of new shares to keep the money value of the issued capital at the same level. Take an example. A company may have shares with a nominal, or par, value of £1. They trade at £3.90 in the market. That company can split the £1 shares into ten, each with 10p nominal value. The shareholders get new certificates. Suddenly the share price is divided by ten, and falls to 39p. Investors are no worse off, because they have ten shares trading at 39p for every one at £3.90 previously. All of a sudden, though, the market has a new penny stock which might attract a fresh wave of investors. That sends the price to, say, 44p, and everyone is pleased. The original investors now have £4.40 for every share which used to sell at £3.90. Terrific.

Similar arithmetic applies to a scrip issue, or capitalisation issue to give it the fancy accounting name. A company which has accumulated sufficient reserves from past profits can give shareholders extra shares – for nothing. In reality, that is just what is being given away – nothing. Because the shareholders own the company, they already owned those reserves anyway. A scrip issue simply changes their position in accounting terms.

In share price impact, however, the move can be very welcome. The company may choose to double the number of shares in issue by giving one new share for every one held. All that happens is that investors find they have twice as many shares as before, but the market price has halved. Once again, though, because investors like lower-priced shares, and because a scrip issue is normally the sign of a confident company, the price often goes up. Share trading profits are conjured out of thin air. No wonder the call for a scrip issue is one of the most frequent shareholder requests at annual company meetings.

Whether they like to admit it or not, most investors are closet penny share punters. I have sat with some of the biggest money men in the land, debating share values. Time and again, with a little grin, the weight of the share price comes up. Fund managers at the biggest, most conservative investment houses know the game. They could not admit to anything so frivolous as a speculation, but they have been around. They know that the lighter the price, the faster it tends to move. They know a share under 100p has more small investor appeal than one over £5. On its own, of course, it is not enough to prompt them to buy. But they know it will help. News that shares are to be split, or made more marketable by a scrip issue, is enough to shift the price higher. And no experienced share trader, large or small, questions the logic of such a move.

The Other Investment Basics

Getting the hang of par values, share splits and scrip issues gives you a handy start on understanding what shares are about. But there is a lot more jargon in the investment business. You do not need to understand it all – like backing a horse, you only need a little cash and a name, not a check on whether all four legs are working – but it can help. The basics are quite simple, really. Whenever they seem too complicated, ask a stockbroker for the answer. Brokers may forget it sometimes, but they are in business to help you, their customer. Never forget it, no matter how superior they may seem, and how apprehensive you may feel. Unfortunately, though, decent broking advice is likely to involve some extra cost these days.

In an earlier edition of this book, I also suggested you might consult your investment adviser. Sadly, too many of the so-called investment adviser firms turned out to be simply excuses to shunt dud shares on to unsophisticated punters. There are some honest operators, but you need to treat investment advisers with extreme caution. Never buy shares they try to sell you. But if you do find one you like, use them to advise you on the shares you are considering.

It is crucial that you do not get into anything you feel uneasy about. It is one thing deliberately deciding you do not want to know, and taking upon yourself the responsibility for operating in the dark. But it is fatal to blunder about only understanding half of what you think you need to know. Never be afraid to ask questions, no matter how elementary they may seem.

Over the years, I have had contact with thousands of investors, and it never ceases to surprise me how little some understand, no matter how successful they have been in other areas. It is a damaging reflection on how the financial press, and the investment community, is doing its job, and is one of the things which has encouraged me to write investment books.

At the same time, I have been impressed by the sheer common sense of most people. Sometimes they come up with questions which floor me – questions which have never occurred to me. Like others in the business, I sometimes get too wrapped up in the investment world each day. I know what the questions mean, but stopping to think about them, and framing answers in a coherent fashion can sometimes be difficult. The problem is usually mine, not the questioner's. Ask away, regardless. The question which seems obvious for you to ask, so obvious that you hesitate to put it, may go straight to the heart of the problem.

Never feel foolish about asking. And keep asking until you get an answer you understand. If, in the end, you cannot get the grip of things, walk away. Either your adviser is not good enough, or not suitable for you. Or whatever you were thinking of doing is not right for you. If it turns out wrong, and you did not realise what you were doing, you have only yourself to blame – and your own money to lose.

Profit Statements

The most routine news you will come across when you look at a share is the company's statement of profits. This comes twice a year from most companies (a few big boys issue quarterly statements, but these hardly figure with penny shares).

The interim statement reports progress for the first half of the company's year. That can run from any date the company chooses. Because the tax year runs to early April, many companies set their year-end at 31 March. Retail businesses often go for 31 January, so they can pull in the results from January sales as well as the Christmas shopping spree. The date does not matter much. The figures even out over the years, though you should watch when companies change year-ends. Sometimes that gives them room for tricky accounting, postponing the day when they have to own up to trouble. A stores company, for example, which changes year-ends and so puts two Christmases into one change-over period will obviously report results which look good at first glance. The mere fact that it is making such a change is suspicious. Perhaps it needs to cover something up, and buy time.

In the normal routine, there will be an unaudited indication of first-half profits, and there should also be news of how business is going. Sometimes there will be an indication of the profits the chairman is expecting for the full year. Sometimes first-half profits will be very different to those for the full year, because the business may be seasonal.

Increasingly, the bigger companies are giving some preliminary guidance on progress about two months before the year-end. They are not allowed to talk about such things in the 'close' period as their year-end approaches, but many like to keep the market informed. That used to mean they told their stockbrokers. Nowadays, thankfully, more of them are being forced to make a general announcement to everyone. Once again, though, this may not happen with too many penny share companies.

What are Profits?

Profits are not always what they seem. Most profit announcements will give sales or turnover. Take off what those sales have cost (the normal running costs), and you get trading profits. These will usually be struck before taking off any interest the company has had to pay on borrowings, or before adding the benefit of any interest earned on any cash in the company. There may also be a minus to cover depreciation, the cash set aside each year as machines and such wear out, so that there will be something in the kitty to buy replacements.

Trading profits usually come, too, after an item called minority interests. These crop up where the company owns part of another business, and so part of the sales and profits belong to the other partner or shareholders. If this part-owned operation made a profit, there will be a deduction from the main group's trading profit to square it up. But if it made a loss, then there will be an addition to group trading profits, because part of the losses falls upon the outside shareholders or partners.

If the company has an employee profit-sharing scheme – which is increasingly popular – the money due to that will be taken out at this point, too. Normally, this only features in full-year figures. Like several of the items which make up the profit and loss account, such a detail will often not be apparent until you get hold of the formal report and accounts.

Pre-tax profits come below trading profits in most statements, though sometimes the two are the same. Pre-tax profits are most commonly used in any discussion of figures, though in many ways the most important figure of all is the net profit, which comes through after deducting tax and dividends due to holders of Preference shares, if there are any.

Most investors, and almost all penny share players, are interested in Ordinary shares, the widely traded and most numerous shares which carry the right to a tiny piece of the company and a proportion of the dividends. Broadly speaking, those dividends rise and fall in line with profits. But some companies have Preference shares, usually entitled to a fixed dividend each year, and with preference over Ordinary shareholders in grabbing a piece of the assets if a business should hit trouble and be wound up.

Net profits after tax and Preference dividends show just how much is left to be paid to shareholders in dividends. This is sometimes translated into earnings per share – or how many pence of profit has been made on behalf of each share. This is a vital figure for investment analysts, and one of the most important of all in comparing the merits of different shares, though it tends to be less significant for penny share companies.

Few companies pay out all of their available profits in dividends, preferring to plough some back into the business. Struggling companies sometimes pay out every penny, or even draw upon reserves to pay the dividend. That is intended to impress shareholders that business is not really so bad, and things will be on the right track next year. Be careful.

Extraordinary and Exceptional Items

The whole profits picture is sometimes influenced by a remarkable pair of gems

– extraordinary profits, and exceptional items. These take us into the wonderful world of creative accounting, and the way in which profits can be made to seem whatever the directors can persuade the auditors is allowable. There are limits, of course, but there is considerable discretion for the inventive finance director or chairman who wants to play games – and many do.

The full repertoire is too large and too tricky for most professionals to keep track of all that goes on. It has attracted such controversy in recent years that the accounting bodies have changed the rules. And they keep changing them, in some ways making life more confusing than ever – though they are trying to help.

Nowadays, extraordinary items are brought into declared profits and appear above the line showing net profits after tax available for Ordinary shareholders. Exceptional profits get the same treatment.

The broad notion is that events and transactions which fall outside the normal activities of a company, and which are not expected to happen frequently or regularly, should be treated as extraordinary. Because of this unusual nature, there is a notion that they need not be allowed to spoil the profits record by making a steady growth pattern look erratic.

Most frequently, the costs of closing factories, paying redundancies and such are treated as extraordinary items. Never forget that these are real costs, and real money has gone out of the company. Whatever they are called, you need to watch out for one-off items, and make appropriate allowances.

More controversially, companies have been using a form of merger accounting to create special provisions for sorting out businesses they have bought. What would otherwise have looked like losses from these newly acquired operations have been written off against these provisions. They can then be written back into profits over the next few years, sometimes making the on-going trading profits look better than they really are. Tighter accounting rules are beginning to make this more difficult.

Exceptional items are also unusual profit and loss events. Perhaps they derive from selling part of the business, selling a factory, or some other asset. Though they may not happen again – you can only sell your factory once – they get slapped in with normal, year-in, year-out profits, helping keep the growth record going in a tricky year.

Extraordinary or exceptional items are now up front in the main profit and loss statement, where you can make up your own mind about them. Whatever their merits, they are the most obvious evidence that profits are not always what they seem.

The warning was clear to anyone who took the trouble to analyse the Maxwell accounts (as I did for years in the *Daily Mail*). The masses from the chattering classes proclaimed, after he had gone, that they knew all along that he was bent. But most kept remarkably quiet about it while he was still up and running, if they really understood. Maxwell demonstrated that a sufficiently determined villain could talk his way around accounting standards and pull the wool over the eyes of most investors for quite some time – though in the end, a bad business will simply run out of money to pay bankers, suppliers, dividends to shareholders, and anyone else.

Accounting Policies

If there are clues to spotting accounting games, you may sometimes spot them in the statement of accounting policies. That precedes the notes in company accounts. Read it. Watch out for anything which refers to capitalised interest or costs. This means the company is not charging certain expenses (cost of borrowing, or building new plant or such) against profits. It is treating it as an addition to assets, and adding it to tangible assets. This is a way of turning a minus (the cost of something) into a plus (writing up asset value), and relieving the profit and loss account of a charge while adding it to the less-publicised reserves. It can be valid in certain circumstances, but watch out. Somebody may be unduly concerned about making things look better than they really are.

Dividends

Most companies pay two dividends each year, the interim or half-time dividend, and the final, or full-year dividend. The final is often larger than the interim. Some companies simply pay only one dividend, at the end of the year. In theory, the year-end dividend has to be approved at the annual meeting, when shareholders will also be asked to vote formal approval of the company's report and accounts.

Dividend Cheques

Cheques for the final dividend are normally posted shortly after the annual meeting, but there are no firm rules on this, nor on when interim dividend cheques are sent out. The dates can vary from year to year, and are worth watching. A late cheque could be a warning that your company is short of cash and is hanging on to what it has got for as long as possible.

The Accounts

The accounts must be sent to shareholders at least 21 days before the annual meeting. Later, I will examine the contents in more detail because the balance sheet in particular can be vital in assessing the worth of penny share companies. Preliminary results are called 'preliminary' because, in theory, they may not yet have been certified by the auditors. It is rare for figures to be altered between the preliminary statement and the report and accounts. If they are, it usually means trouble.

Auditors' Report

If the figures are amended, it will be because the auditors have unearthed something unexpected, or have not resolved an argument with the directors over how certain matters should be presented to shareholders. All accounts contain an auditors' report, normally certifying that the financial statements present a true and fair view of the state of affairs, and conform to the Companies Act. This report seems to get longer each year, without really adding much value.

The auditors are a firm of accountants, technically responsible not to the directors, but to shareholders, who have to go through the motion of approving their pay at the annual meeting each year. The auditors are meant to verify that the figures are what they say they are, that there has been no jiggery-pokery to mislead shareholders. In practice, there is a vast range of allowable accounting options open to directors in deciding just what a profit may be.

So long, though, as the board operates within the accounting rules, they can get a clean bill of health from the auditors. If there is a massive disagreement between board and auditors, the auditors signal it by qualifying their report in some way. Almost anything which departs from the routine declaration of a true and fair view is a warning to shareholders.

Watch especially for any note which says the continued operation as a going concern depends on anything – that means the company is running out of cash, and someone could pull the rug away if they ask for their loans back. If the auditors say they cannot form an opinion, or that the accounts do not conform to the Companies Act, the business really is in trouble. Only if the auditors say they agree with the way in which the company has not complied with the Companies Act can you breathe again.

Voting Powers

The accounts will contain a list of the resolutions to be put to shareholders at the annual meeting. They normally cover the re-election of a few directors (some must stand down each year), and there will probably be a clause asking for approval to issue extra shares without going first to the existing shareholders. Whether you attend or not, you should be sent a form of proxy, allowing you to register your vote. All shareholders have a vote, unless they have bought non-voting shares. There are some of these, but the Stock Exchange frowns on them, and they are gradually being phased out.

The Directors' Report

Company reports are getting ever glossier, but they incorporate a routine report from the directors, giving details of their own shareholdings, their options to buy shares, any changes in them during the year, and the identity of anyone holding over 3% of the company. It also shows any dealings between the directors and the company, plus contributions to charities or political parties.

The Chairman's Statement

The chairman's statement is a central feature of any report and accounts, giving the boss a chance to sound off. Nowadays, most concentrate on the progress of the company during the year, with a break-down of profits and sales between the main activities, and by geographical area. Increasingly, there is an additional message from the chief executive, and occasionally from divisional directors. They are all worth studying. They rarely convey any exciting information, but give a valuable impression of what the company is up to, and the manner in which it is being run. That impression matters – sometimes more than the figures themselves. Everybody will know the same figures, but each individual investor will depend upon his own interpretation of the message from the directors to assess the company's progress.

Corporate Governance

These days, all accounts contain a section dealing with corporate governance, the Cadbury Committee, or the Greenbury report on pay. A few companies have the nerve to say that they do not comply with Cadbury, and do not have sufficient non-executive directors or something. In many ways, these are the interesting companies, run by people with nerve enough to stand out from the herd.

Almost everyone, though, will now be anxious to assure shareholders that they meet the generally approved standards for running the business, with a full complement of non-executive directors, a split between chairman and chief executive roles, a proper remuneration committee, and so on. For the most part, it is meaningless irrelevance, adding extra cost and giving the board extra excuses if something goes wrong. And, perhaps, the chance to invite a few old pals onto the gravy train as non-executives. Sensible investors will pay little attention to this self-serving nonsense, and concentrate on profits and progress to form their own conclusions about whether the company is being run properly.

Annual Meetings

If you can, you should go to the annual meeting. Shareholders do not have to attend, and many companies rarely have more than half a dozen people in the room – friends of the directors, or advisers. Increasingly, however, annual meetings are becoming real events. Some companies attract hundreds of shareholders, put on a show, and provide drinks and snacks. Many offer food, some give away samples, or display new products with someone on hand to discuss them.

Like the annual report, the meetings give an invaluable opportunity not just to get a feel of how the company operates, but what the men in charge are really like. It is the only time in the year when investors can demand answers of their board. They may not get them. Some company chairmen restrict questions tightly to matters relating to the report and accounts, others allow the meeting to range far and wide into irrelevant areas. Marks & Spencer shareholders are notorious for pursuing complaints about the shade of the socks at their local stores. The board is probably grateful to deal with such trivia instead of matters of more substance.

When you buy shares, you are backing individuals, a chairman and his fellow directors. You need to weigh them up, form your own conclusions. If you want to ask a question, do it politely and briefly. Do not make a speech, and do not ramble. But do listen to the answer. If it dodges your question, try to pursue a proper answer, firmly. Do not be daunted by the occasion. The chairman will often be every bit as nervous as you are. Many company men are uncomfortable in front of an audience, and it may be the only time of the year when they can be caught on the hop, cannot duck awkward questions, and have to satisfy someone who need not defer to their answer.

If you get the chance, stay after the meeting, and chat to directors. It often surprises me the care and attention very powerful and busy men give to shareholders – even the odd crackpot – when they meet them. Seize any chance to get a better feel of what is afoot. But be careful not to confuse glossiness and slick presentation with real efficiency. And do be suspicious of companies which hold meetings at awkward times, in awkward places. They may have something to hide.

Extraordinary Meetings

For penny share companies, extraordinary meetings may well be more important than annual meetings. It may take extreme devotion to get to them. They may yield nothing. But you might just find them the most valuable events in your investment life.

Extraordinary meetings are called whenever a company has to put some major change to shareholders, and gain their approval. Extraordinary meetings take place virtually every time a new team moves in to shake up a company. They mark the beginning of a new era for many penny share companies. The new boys will be there, nervous, and usually expecting few shareholders to be present. What better time to nobble them, and chat about their hopes for their new company – your penny share company?

You can pass up the chance, of course. Whatever will happen is going to happen with, or without your approval. But you will have a much clearer idea in your own mind of the abilities of the management, and how the company's future may unfold. Formal explanation of what is afoot will appear in the document which will have been sent seeking your support. Stock Exchange regulations – intended to clarify and to protect the unwitting investor from over-optimistic projections – often mean that little of the real game plan can be displayed in the documents. Later, I show how you can unravel what these documents really mean. But a face-to-face chat might put a very different complexion on things. You can sometimes wheedle out the most remarkable details of what is going on behind the scenes. Do try to do it.

Presentation

Among penny share companies, especially, elaborate efforts at presentation should be viewed with suspicion. All too often, by the time they are shouting about what they may do, the real share gains have happened. The boys who spotted what was afoot when the company looked a clapped-out no-hoper have made the big killing, and want out.

By and large, penny share companies do not have the resources to make too much of a public relations effort. Video reports on where the business is going, glossy accounts fat with colour photographs of the chairman and board, free samples galore at the annual meeting, and perks to shareholders all cost money. Giant companies can afford it. They have the turnover to carry the expense, though it is questionable – even for some of them.

A slick presentation from a smaller company can be encouraging because it demonstrates that the directors are concerned to impress investors. And if they are out to impress investors, they are working to get their share price up – just what the shareholder wants.

Ask yourself why, though. Ask yourself if they are going too far, trying too hard. Ponder whether they are spending time, thought and money on the way things look when they should be spending it on the core of the business. Have they really got their eye on the ball? Are they trying to boost the shares so they can make an acquisition with their inflated paper? When they buy another business, will they really get down to their shirt sleeves and understand how to cope with it? Are they getting ready to sell out themselves? Have they fallen in love with their own publicity? Are they making a dash for a quick killing?

These questions are not born of simple bloody-mindedness. You want your company to be noticed, because the more people who buy the shares, the higher the price should rise. So you need to strike a sensible balance. Through the years, some of the slickest-looking operations I have seen have also turned out to be some of the emptiest.

In a small company – a penny share-type company – the bigger the noise, the greater the risk, perhaps. The rule is not infallible. No investment rules are. But be warned. And be doubly warned if you are dealing with a company which does not have a full Stock Exchange listing. There are some outstanding opportunities among shares traded on the Alternative Investment Market, and maybe even some very high-risk bargains among the Ofex off-market trades. But you need to be very sure you know what you are doing. If not, you are not just playing with fire. You could be sitting on a time-bomb.

You are on the way, starting to speak the language, understanding the evidence. Are you feeling ready to buy some shares?

FOUR

Where Do You Buy Penny Shares?

Whether time-bombs ticking away, ready to explode in your face, or stock market rockets, ready to soar to the skies, penny shares are all around. Finding them is no great problem. Share prices are everywhere. Pick up almost any newspaper and you will find a list. Some of them are bound to be penny shares. No matter how popular the sector may get, how many buyers push prices up, there are always companies on the way down, with prices sliding into the penny class. That kind of action created many new penny shares in the late Nineties. The problem is sorting the good from the bad, sifting those which are going to go up from the ones which will carry on down.

Or perhaps you will end up sorting out the ones which have got a chance from those which are doomed before you buy them. In good times, when the market is booming, there tend to be many basically unsound companies masquerading as potential winners. That is the time, too, when naive punters are plagued by share pushing firms, singing the praises of rubbish share certificates, not worth the paper they are printed on, perhaps even churned out on some printing press outside this country, flogged by slick salesmen reciting from a craftily prepared script.

If you are new to the share business, you are at your most vulnerable. Your interest makes you easy meat for crooks who prey on unsophisticated, inexperienced investors, and steal their money by selling them dud or near-worthless shares. Before you start, you need to know where to go to buy, who will give you a fair deal, and who will rook you. That is why it is important to spend a little time learning how the different markets work, how to tell one from another, and how to tell a straight share salesman from a bent one.

The Stock Exchange

It is easy to criticise the London Stock Exchange. It sometimes treats the small investor in the most unsympathetic fashion. The machinery creaks and groans, allows the most extraordinary cheating to go unpunished, and lends an air of respectability to all manner of dubious propositions. Nonetheless, it means well. It is the best stock market I know, operates in the fairest fashion of those I have seen, and tries to give the sucker something like an even break.

Most members of the London Stock Exchange are reasonable and honest. That is not to say that they will not try to get the best of any deal for themselves. Of course they will. Big money, the right connections and knowing how close you can sail to the wind always gives advantages to insiders in any such organisation. But most Stock Exchange members play by the rules, and acquit themselves in an honourable enough fashion, with a sense of responsibility. The rules the Exchange lays down for those who trade there, and the companies whose shares they trade in, are sound and sensible, by and large. If you want to buy a share, go first for a company with a listing on the London Stock Exchange, and buy it through a member of the Stock Exchange. There is no better way.

How to Find a Broker

Finding a stockbroker is a major headache for small investors, new and old. In theory, there ought not to be much problem. In practice, unfortunately, it seems to be a mine-field.

The easiest way used to be to write to the Stock Exchange at The Public Affairs Department, The Stock Exchange, London, EC2N 1HP. They used to have all sorts of useful things to send you, free of charge, but then abandoned the idea for a while. Last time I tried, however, they were back in positive mode, and did have some handy booklets. There is no guarantee that they will still be bothering about small investors when you try, but you might be lucky. They have tried to shunt most such things off to others. Most useful is the Association of Private Client Investment Managers and Stockbrokers, or APCIMS. That publishes a directory listing stockbroking firms who specialise in dealing with the smaller, private investor. It gives their names, addresses and telephone numbers. Contact APCIMS at 112, Middlesex Street, London, E1 7HY (phone 0171-247 7080).

Obviously, circumstances change, but I have tried a small, random test. It worked well, and I was most impressed by the helpful way I was treated by brokers who had no means of knowing who I was, or that I was simply testing. This is no guarantee, of course, that we would have got on when it actually came to trading, but it encourages me to feel that small traders can get a fair deal, especially among stockbrokers outside London, where the pressure is less, overheads are lower, and there is more time for the personal touch.

There is also ProShare, an organisation which is part-sponsored by the Stock Exchange and exists to encourage the private investor. It does publish several useful guides, but never quite seems to know what it is doing from month to month, and the addresses seem to change. Contact ProShare at PO Box 1, Hastings, TN35 4SE or phone 0424 755755. Or you might do better at their City address: Library Chambers, 13-14 Basinghall Street, London, EC2V 5BQ. Unless they have changed it, the best bet might to be to look on the internet for their web site at www.proshare.org.uk.

If you fail to get real help at these semi-official bodies (they seem to be dogged by internal debates over whether anyone really wants to pay for helping small investors), buy the *Investors Chronicle*. That has no conflict of interest. It exists to help people like you, and depends on you to buy the magazine to keep it going. It runs regular valuable features on all sorts of small investor information.

Otherwise you could try *Yellow Pages*, or resort to the traditional alternative of asking your friends, with a view to finding a broker by personal recommendation or through an introduction. It may work. But broking can be a very personal business. You may not find you get along. You could find you are passed on to a junior member of the firm. That could have advantages. He might be keen to impress, to advance his career, and you might benefit from his enthusiasm. On the other hand, his inexperience may mean you do not get the kind of advice you would like. As a new investor, the blind could be leading the blind. A more senior member with less time to spare might serve you better.

Execution-Only Brokers

These days, many broking firms advertise what appear to be cheap dealing services. Usually, you will find that they are execution-only brokers. This means that they will buy or sell for you on your instructions. They do not offer advice.

They simply execute your deals. They may be highly efficient and reliable – certainly with names like ShareWise – but unless you pay extra, you get nothing extra.

This is not a proper broking relationship in the old style. Firms like ShareWise are worth investigating, however. They have added a wide range of other useful services. Pay extra, and some will give you access to broking research on companies, and much else. Check to see what suits you. On the whole, however, I advise penny share punters to try to strike up a long-term relationship with a broker who will chat to you, and help you along whenever you call. You may pay more in dealing charges, but good advice can be worth a fortune – certainly more than saving a fiver or two here or there on dealing costs. If your broker saves you from just one dud investment, that could be worth hundreds of pounds.

Hordes of small investors also claim they lost a small fortune in the early months of 2000 when they found they simply could not get through to their execution-only brokers. Tales of hanging on the phone line for ninety minutes or more while volatile prices roared up and down were everywhere. In fairness, traditional brokers were also overwhelmed at times, though there were fewer really serious complaints.

On-Line Brokering

Thanks to the internet explosion, it is now possible to deal on-line. At the click of a button, the theory is that you can buy or sell shares in an instant without having the bother of talking to anyone. In theory, it is fine. In practice, many would-be on-line investors have found that they are left hanging on, waiting to get through, when they most need to get into the action. And systems crash for various reasons.

Do not assume on-line broking is the answer to your prayers. It will take a while for the system to bed down. But it could be good for many stocks, and might be cheaper. Both execution-only and on-line brokers got in such a tangle with the paperwork early in 2000 that many stopped dealing in so-called "residual" stocks. These are shares in companies which are not registered with the Crest paperless certificate system. Because they involve buyers and sellers in having to swap paper certificates, the paperwork for brokers is more complicated and time-consuming. It gets worse if investors delay in posting certificates. This may involve fines being levied on late delivery, so the whole business can be complicated.

Since some residual stocks were great gambling favourites in 2000, that poses another problem for share punters. As more companies switch to Crest, it should disappear. But watch out. Ask before you buy whether your intended purchase is a residual stock or not. Think twice if it is. In busy times, it could be hard to sell.

How to Use your Broker

Whatever you do, do not get upset if your broker starts asking personal questions about your financial position and such. It makes sense. He needs to know what kind of investor you are. He will not want to put you into the wrong kind of investments. There are now laws which actually require investment advisers to know their customers and to refrain from putting them into unsuitable investments. Any broker will need you to fill in quite a detailed client agreement form. Make it clear that you want to play the penny share market, and are ready and able to take a gamble. Some brokers do not approve, and will not wish to take you on. It is no good complaining. Accept it. An unhappy team will never make money together. You need to be able to trust each other. Ideally, your broker will become a valuable friend, and you will both make money.

A good broker will pass on gossip and ideas generated by his firm's research department. Acres of print are churned out by stockbroking analysts, most of them little more than visible justification for the snappy summary which they have already given their biggest and best clients on the telephone. Big boys get first bite, and the best chance of profit.

Research can be invaluable, however. Some of it is excellent, with detailed assessments and explanations of what companies do, and their potential. Ask your broker what is on offer, and study it when you can. It not only tells you about specific companies, but can give you a valuable insight into how to make investment decisions yourself, raising the sort of questions which you might like answered, but never thought to ask.

Block-buster research is not widely available on penny shares. But small brokers are becoming more receptive in this area. There are more and more chatty assessments of opportunities. They may not be bang up to date by the time you get them, but they can be very useful. You do not always have to be in at the very beginning to make a killing in the penny share jungle.

When it actually comes to dealing, give your broker clear instructions. He needs to know whether you wish him to deal 'at best' – the best price he can get for you at the time – or 'on limits'. If you want to trade on limits, lay down what price you will take, and how long you are prepared to wait to get it. Most brokers will not accept limits for an indefinite period, but will keep their eyes open for a week or two. Be prepared to accept responsibility for whatever you say. If you do say 'at best' and end up paying more than you expected because the price has leapt, it is your fault, not your broker's. And if he does not sell because the price never quite reached the level you gave him, and then slumped sharply, it is your fault that you missed out – not his.

If you can be sufficiently self-disciplined, you might find using limits particularly helpful in buying shares in smaller companies where the spread between buying and selling prices is wide. Set a limit near the middle price, and give your broker and the market-maker something to aim for.

Once again, mutual trust is important. If you find a good broker, he might be prepared to deal for you, using his discretion, when you are not around. Sometimes he will make the wrong move. But he is on the spot. If you both accept that he means well, such a relationship should pay off in the end.

Brokers are only human. Most want to do well for their clients, and will be happy when their clients are happy. Just now and then, though, some get tempted when the chips are down. Never give your broker a sum of money and complete discretion to use it as he sees fit. Keep in touch with what is going on. Brokers have been known to push clients into shares they themselves are holding in an effort to move the price up. And where broking houses also act as corporate financiers, advising companies on strategy, they might sometimes find it convenient to persuade individual investment clients to buy because it suits their corporate finance department. Such conflicts of interest are frowned upon, of course. Their existence will be pooh-poohed officially. But they do crop up.

And sometimes, of course, it will be to your advantage that they do. They might be using you to help get a hot stock moving. Just keep your eyes and ears open.

One warning, too, about your broker's gossip. He might tell you he has bought stock himself because he believes in a particular rumour, and that other big investors he knows have been buying. Fine. He might be doing you a favour. But stockbrokers do not pay commission on their trading. They can pop in and out quickly, and make money on a very small margin. You will have to pay dealing commission to your broker, who makes money out of you whether you win or lose. A rise of 1p can mean a winning deal for your broker trading for himself. It might take you a rise of 5p or 6p to break even. And your broker gets that 5p or 6p. So be careful.

The Stock Exchange System

The Stock Exchange system changed radically with the Big Bang in October 1986. One of the major changes was the end of minimum commission charges. Now brokers can charge what they think fit. It means that most smaller investors pay more, and the big boys less – sometimes much less.

Brokers have become more cost-conscious, aware that it takes as much time and paper-work to process a £500 order as it does one for £50,000. Some brokers offer no-frills dealing with a minimum charge of £20 or less. The widely advertised operators, like ShareWise, do a solid job. They simply buy or sell for you, and offer no advice. If you want time and their ideas, you pay more. Once again, though, outside London there are more brokers ready to give you a more personal service.

Agents and Market-Makers

Before Big Bang, a stockbroker was simply your agent. He acted for you, buying or selling shares on your behalf, using a jobber. A jobber was a sort of share wholesaler who never dealt directly with the public, but would hold blocks of shares which he would trade with brokers, moving the price up as demand rose, reducing it when he was hit by more sellers and might have been left holding more stock than he wanted. Not too different from some shops, really.

Now, though, market-makers perform the jobbing function. They agree to quote prices for minimum quantities of particular shares, and to buy or sell on that basis. They show their prices on SEAQ, the Stock Exchange Automated Quotations system, available on screens in every broker's office. Inside six months, this system made the old Stock Exchange floor redundant. It closed completely early in 1992. Face-to-face dealing is out. Telephone calls based on screen prices dominate. Brokers who were brilliant at reading a jobber's face, chatting their way around his defences to wring an extra penny or two out of him, now feel lost. The new dealing kings have quick fingers on the button.

Everyone in the market can see the same prices at the same time. Thereafter, it is a matter of getting through on the phone – something which favours the big names, who have direct lines into the main market-makers, who will pick up the phone to talk to them before they will answer calls from the also-rans.

For individual investors, though, the main change is that some brokers are now also market-makers. They themselves may be holding the shares you want to buy or sell. In theory, they are required to deal for you to your best advantage, regardless of their position. In practice, big investors who are well aware of this have learnt to use or ignore such brokers as they think it might suit their situation. You, too, will need to decide for yourself whether to worry about the potential conflict of interest.

Some broking firms have deliberately chosen not to become market-makers, and simply act as agency brokers in the old style, not holding shares on their own account. This has won them support from some investment houses. For the small investor, however, the difference probably does not matter too much. Your broker ought to tell you if his firm has a position in the shares you want to trade, and you can react accordingly.

The Paperwork

Once you have found your broker, the paperwork is the same, whoever you go to. The day he deals for you, or the next day, he will post a contract note to you. The charges were discussed in the earlier chapter when we were taking a look at the disadvantages of playing penny shares. Buying or selling, you pay the broker's commission, plus VAT at 17%. If you have bought, there is also stamp duty at .5% of the purchase value. Deals over £5,000 attract a 60p levy to help pay the costs of regulating the market.

Keep the contract note. You may have to show it to the Inland Revenue when you send in your capital gains tax return. It also shows settlement date, the day when you pay your broker or he pays you. The Stock Exchange used to run on an account system, with accounts running for two or three weeks, normally ending on a Friday. Settlement was six working days after the end of the account. If you had done a series of deals in the account, your broker would set off the pluses and minuses, and one cheque would be due.

If you bought and sold again in the same account, you simply collected a cheque for your winnings, or sent one to cover your loss. If you could spot rapid price movements, you could do very well. Get it wrong, though, and you could lose a lot more than you bargained for.

Like so many things which attracted the small client, the Stock Exchange has now done away with account trading. Buy now and both sides are supposed to settle five days after the deal was done – 'T plus 5' in the official lingo. This means you cannot buy and sell again before paying. It also means you have to deal with correspondence promptly, sending share certificates quickly to your broker after selling. If you do not settle five days after trading, you may be charged interest on the cash you owe.

Many investors find this impossible and inconvenient. It is possible to deal T plus 10, or T plus 25, if you first agree it with your broker. That means you pay 10 or 25 days after trading. To do so, you may pay extra. You may well have to pay a little more for shares you want to buy on that basis, or accept a little less if you sell for distant settlement.

It is still possible, dealing T plus 25, to sell before you have paid, and emerge with a clear profit without putting up the actual cash for buying. Alternatively, some brokers have developed banking arrangements which allow you to deal on margin. Effectively, this commits you to putting up a certain amount of capital, and borrowing the rest. It is not to be recommended, except for relatively wealthy, sophisticated traders. And it may be difficult to do in many penny shares.

Nominee Accounts

Because of the need to have easy access to share certificates, many brokers are urging clients to deal in nominee accounts. This means that the shares you buy are registered in the name of the broker's nominee. All documents are sent to the nominee, not to you.

In theory, your shares should be perfectly safe, whatever happens. In practice, if a broker hits trouble, there is often a muddle over nominee accounts. It can takes months to sort out. Sometimes, there are too few shares to satisfy all nominee account holders. Any such shortfall is covered by the Investors' Compensation Scheme. But that only runs to £48,000 out of the first £50,000. So, for big players, it has limitations. Crucially, some brokers charge extra for sending on documents to the nominee account holders. So you will not automatically get the annual report and accounts from your company, unless you pay extra. And you might not be entitled to attend company meetings and vote without paying extra. Indeed, you might not be able to vote at all.

This is a contentious subject. Officialdom is eager to assure everyone that investors will not suffer through nominee accounts. That may be so in some cases but I do not accept that it is so in many cases. You may want to insist that any shares you buy are registered directly in your name. Then you know, for certain, where you stand – although you do have to keep track of share certificates and will be involved in extra paperwork.

Ex and Cum

Brokers might want your shares handy for them in a nominee account, but even when you have sold a share, that may not be quite the last you hear of it. For several weeks, you may continue to receive documents, even dividends. They may not belong to you.

Dividends normally go to whoever owns the shares at the time they are announced, not when the dividends are actually paid. The shares may be traded 'cum' – with the dividend. They stay that way for a few days after the announcement, then they are traded 'ex' (or without) the dividend for a spell before returning to normal with neither 'ex' or 'cum' against the name. After that point, new buyers get whatever is announced from the moment they buy. Anyone buying 'ex' is not entitled to the recent dividend, though the cheque may not actually be sent out for weeks, perhaps months.

The same rules apply to things like scrip and rights issues. If the shares trade normally, or 'cum', you get whatever is about. When you buy them 'ex', you do not. If you get a dividend cheque you are not entitled to, pay it into your account, and wait for your broker to ask for a cheque from you for him to pass along to the new, rightful, owner.

There is one more interested party, too – the Inland Revenue. Whenever you get a dividend cheque, it comes after deduction of tax at standard rate. Anyone who pays tax at higher rates will have to account for the extra tax at the end of the tax year.

The Alternative Investment Market

It all works the same way, whether you buy shares with a full Stock Exchange listing or on the Alternative Investment Market. Both are covered by the official Stock Exchange rules, and can be traded by members of the Stock Exchange.

Known as AIM, the Alternative Investment Market opened for business on 19 June 1995. I have called it the opportunity market in my book *How To Make A Killing On The Alternative Investment Market*. It is home to many penny shares.

The intention is to create a more lightly regulated exchange to cater for younger, smaller, growing companies. The idea is that they should be able to raise risk capital more easily and cheaply, without going through all of the hoops required of a bigger business coming to the full market. The Exchange itself does not vet the companies and their documents, but leaves it to the nominated advisers who effectively sponsor the company as it gains an AIM quotation. All companies must have a nominated adviser. Most are stockbrokers, but there are some accountants and other investment firms.

The Exchange monitors it all and undertakes pretty strict vetting of the advisers. It has excluded many of the more controversial veterans and tightened up quite significantly after a few nasty episodes in the first 18 months. Unfortunately, that does not mean that the AIM is absolutely safe for the small investor, but then nothing in the share world manages that.

I have devoted a whole book to trying to explain the pitfalls and the possibilities. There have been outstanding opportunities for making money, but the risks have been quite high. A few quite ludicrous flotations have crept through the net, demonstrating that officialdom can always be fooled.

AIM companies are generally smaller and more speculative than others. Because some are start-ups, and others quite new, there is a risk that they will not develop into viable businesses, and could go bust relatively quickly. Some are in the exploration business, which always makes me uncomfortable. Others are run by people with dubious records, or have villains hovering in the background. When they issue documents to raise money, the Exchange insists that all AIM directors must list other companies where they are on the board, and their directorships over the past five years. They must also list unspent convictions, companies which have crashed while they were on the board or within 12 months of their departure, and any public criticisms by statutory or regulatory authorities. That makes it important to try to get hold of any relevant documents before investing in an AIM company. You would prefer to know, wouldn't you, if you were backing a business run by someone whose last two ventures went belly-up?

Best place to go for the documents is the registered office of the company itself, or the nominated adviser. You could also try the nominated broker – sometimes the same as the nominated adviser – or ask your broker to check with the market-maker in the stock.

AIM shares are listed on a special section of the stock market screen services. There are usually only two or three market-makers (usually J.P. Jenkins or Winterflood Securities), and it may not always be easy to trade in reasonable quantities. Check, and never deal in larger amounts than the market norm. If you do, you could find problems in selling for any reasonable price.

There are some readily tradeable stocks, however, with a pretty lively market in several of the leading contenders.

AIM Illustrative Projections

Though there are dangers in the AIM, there are advantages. For the small investor, stumbling through the fine print without a stockbroking analyst to assist, the most useful innovation was the illustrative profit projection. This featured in early AIM prospectuses. Fearful that over-eager promoters would lure unsuspecting investors in with rosy projections, the Stock Exchange does not allow fully listed companies to publish profit forecasts, unless they are short-term. For a while, it was different on AIM.

Some companies took advantage of the opportunity to show projections for three years ahead. These were not, strictly speaking, forecasts. But they came as close as they could, accompanied by a note from the auditors certifying that they followed consistent guide-lines.

They were most useful. Usually they projected sales and profits, with detailed cash flow and such, a map of where the business might go. Crucially, they showed how earnings might advance over the next three years, giving you an idea of how much hope value you were buying.

Typically, however, the heavy hand of the Stock Exchange dropped on these after several companies had fallen massively short of their projections. Rather than risk getting it wrong, most new companies now opt not to give projections. You may find a few still, especially in smaller issues which are not planning an AIM quote but are looking at the Ofex (more of that later). You must remember that they are only illustrative projections, and cannot be taken as carved in stone. But they do give you a useful guide.

Because there are so few now, this section may appear irrelevant to most companies. But they are valuable if you buy later into a company which issued projections at the beginning. Seek them out. Then you can see how accurate they have proved, and get some idea of how reliable management comments may be. Because projections may only be in the initial prospectus, it is important to try to get hold of that document.

Tax Breaks

AIM companies could have other advantages. The tax man may help. Initially, the Inland Revenue agreed that AIM shares would not be treated as quoted or listed for tax purposes. This meant that shares in a qualifying company were eligible for roll-over relief for capital gains tax. So if you sold an AIM share and re-invested the proceeds in another qualifying company (perhaps another AIM issue) within three years, you did not pay tax on the original gain. Effectively, you could play with part of the tax man's money.

In addition, it was possible to offset losses on qualifying AIM companies against income tax. Majority owners of AIM companies could also be eligible for relief from inheritance tax.

Inevitably, this sensible rule, which encouraged investors into small companies, has since come under threat. Now only the smallest companies qualify, and the whole position has become unclear. It may yet change back. But it is important to check first if you are interested in these tax reliefs. It is folly to undertake any investment for tax reasons alone. Look on the possible tax breaks as a possible added advantage, but select your share on investment merit alone.

Penny AIMs

It is worth devoting so much attention to the AIM simply because many of the companies which come to AIM fall into the penny share class. They are often high-risk, high-return investments. That said, there is no reason to treat AIM penny shares much differently to the rest when it comes to deciding what to buy. The advice in this book applies equally well to AIM shares or fully-listed ones – except that there may be more sharks swimming closer to the surface in AIM stocks, and that the best AIM issues could just be sensational winners, if they work. They could go bust more easily.

Ofex

As the Stock Exchange has shunted the system around frequently over the past 15 years, by default it has created the need for some way of trading shares in the very smallest start-up companies, or those which do not really want a full listing. So John Jenkins, who made his name as a respected market-maker under the old system, has developed the Ofex as a means for trading in such companies. It has become home to a few hundred businesses, generally smaller companies, or big ones whose shares change hands less frequently. There are a few really big names – companies like Weetabix, or National Parking (until it was subject to an £800m takeover in 1998).

In some cases, Ofex is likely to take in businesses which have not been able to find a suitable supporter ready to act as a nominated adviser and thus gain the seal of approval to move up to the AIM, or obtain a full listing. There will be yet other companies which find the costs of AIM too great. They may be businesses wanting to raise a few hundred thousand pounds, reluctant to pay £150,000 or more to do it. Inevitably, as AIM has developed, the red tape has multiplied, and costs with it. By 1998, many advisers were saying it cost as much to go onto AIM as to get a full listing. That means some very small and exciting companies are being traded off-market. They plan to sit there for a few years, getting used to the idea of public shareholders, limbering up before they can move to the Stock Exchange. One or two have gone from Ofex to a full listing. There will be more. Spotting them early can be highly rewarding. I have found a small number of big Ofex winners – Robotic Technology, National Parking, Knowledge Management Software and turbo Genset – for *Mail* readers. But Ofex is home to several of the kind of companies investors should avoid.

Until you really know what you are doing, stay clear of Ofex. The regulations are deliberately low-key, and listing costs cheap. Tread warily in any kind of market outside the Stock Exchange – even that widely televised Nasdaq US market contains hundreds of nasty little companies. In the UK, the Department of Trade is effectively the regulator of last resort. As anyone who was conned into putting money with the fraudulent Barlow Clowes empire knows, having the Department of Trade as a regulator is like asking Robert Maxwell to keep an eye on your pension fund.

Crooks and Cheats

In the Eighties, there was an active over-the-counter market, where boys outside the Stock Exchange floated companies and made a market in the shares. Now, this is dead. The nearest you may get is telephone selling by crooks and cheats of shares which they claim are traded on some overseas market, usually in North America. On no account have anything to do with any of them. Most want to steal your money.

It is illegal for such people to phone out of the blue and try to sell you shares. Cold-calling is the name for it, and there are many tricks used to get around the law against it. One of the most popular used to be to advertise cheap dealing services for privatisation issues. Beware should it spring up again. The cheap trading deals were used to give the hustlers the names of unsophisticated investors who had a little money which they were willing to use to dabble in shares. Once you sell a respectable issue, never let any dealer persuade you to use the cash to buy anything else.

Beware, as well, of broking houses who ring out of the blue with investment ideas in British quoted stocks, or offer free written advice. They may be Stock Exchange members, or have some other regulatory seal of approval. They may do a good job. The chances are, sadly, that they will be trying to sell you shares in small, obscure companies. Often these will be penny shares.

The houses may have bought a large line of them at a discount to the price quoted by Stock Exchange market-makers. The salesman – or woman – will be ready to sell to you at, or even slightly below, the quoted price. The seller will be taking a profit along the way. Sometimes, the shares will be winners. More often, they will be duds. Either way, the main idea will be to earn commission and a dealing profit by selling to you. Helping you make money will be secondary.

Sooner or later, anyone dealing with such houses tends to come a cropper. You might have a good run, and the salesman might appear quite a pal, offering tit-bits of advice and promises of good profit. Even if you do well to start with, you could get sucked into spending more money than you intended. "Churn 'em, and burn 'em" is the motto of many of these boys. They will shunt you in and out of shares, taking their commissions, until your cash is gone – to them. If things go wrong, you could find yourself deep in debt – or owed money by a firm which suddenly hits trouble and is closed down.

Above all, do not sign any document saying you understand the risks unless you really do understand those risks. If anything goes wrong, you will find your chances of getting anything back have been gravely diminished by such foolishness. Some people even sign agreements saying they understand options, and the risks. They rarely do. Yet some find themselves trading massively expensive options in American shares without a glimmer of understanding.

Even if your adviser is trading in shares in respectable companies, check how much commission you are being charged. That could gobble up more of your cash than losing deals. Look suspiciously, too, at any extra charges which are loaded on. Question it if you are charged, say, a penny extra for shares for some reason or other. It happens, and it is a warning sign, even if it is only a penny on a share priced at several pounds.

Quite often, the bucket shops seek to suck you in by the initial offer of a research report on some company in which you hold shares. The share-selling house simply buys a list of shareholders, and mails most of them. The salespeople can be remarkably persistent and persuasive. Do not get lured in. If you are unhappy about what happens to you, contact the Personal Investment Authority. Note what the salespeople say – especially if they promise early news or capital gains. Tape the chat if you are worried. If it all goes wrong, that might help deliver crucial evidence.

The Policemen

If you do get caught by total crooks there is little you can do about it. The offshore ones operate outside the rules, and the law is hopelessly inadequate to deal with them. If they should get caught, your money will be beyond salvation. Send money to anyone working from any address overseas, and you can almost certainly kiss it goodbye.

Stick within the City framework, and you have some hope – but no absolute guarantee. The whole thing keeps changing so much, with self-regulatory bodies shifting offices and areas of authority. It becomes totally confusing. Trying to cope with them drives me mad. Even now, when I come across something which is clearly outrageous, it can take days to hack through the maze of regulators, each quick to shift responsibility to another. Sometimes none of them really wants to know.

If you do get it wrong, your anger and frustration will be compounded when you try to get help from the official bodies. So take all of the care you possibly can. If you have to complain, perhaps the starting point is the Personal Investment Authority on 0171-538 8860. The Personal Investment Authority Ombudsman, if you fall out with the PIA, is on 0171-216 0016. The Securities and Investments Board has a help-line on 0171-929 3652. That may give you a start, and will allow you to check if the dealers are who they say they are and are authorised to do the business for you. There is a Complaints Bureau at the Securities and Futures Association which regulates Stock Exchange members on 0171-676 1000. The Department of Trade and Industry is in the phone book. If you are lucky, you might find a helpful official.

There is no guarantee that, by the time you read this, all of the regulators will not have swapped around and moved into yet more expensive offices. Just keep ringing. One or the other should give you an idea of who to grumble to, eventually.

Dealing with a member of the London Stock Exchange is as near a guarantee of fair play as you will get. It qualifies you for protection under the Investors' Compensation Scheme if your broker goes bust or loses you money by breaking the rules. The ICS covers other properly supervised UK financial advisers. The maximum compensation, sadly, is the first £30,000 in full, and up to 90% of the next £20,000 – effectively a maximum of £48,000 of the first £50,000 of losses. There is nothing thereafter, unless you go to court. Clearly you should not put more than £50,000 with any one adviser.

Use your common sense, and you should not have to trouble any of the investment policemen. Almost always – not every time – the cases I come across result from some degree of carelessness, stupidity, or greed on the part of the investor.

Above all, do not try to cut corners. Do not try to do things on the cheap, risking hundreds of pounds to save a fiver on dealing costs. Opt for safety first, every time, please. You are going to take risks enough playing the penny share game. Do not load the odds against yourself by dealing with anyone you cannot trust completely.

Buying Through Your Bank

The idea of buying shares through your bank used to be a non-starter for serious investors. Day by day, it is becoming more plausible. The big banks are eager to court customers, and see share-dealing services as a good way of doing it.

New ideas are being introduced regularly, and bank branches in bigger towns have screens reporting up-to-the-minute share prices. Local assistants may not be too clued up, however, and though they can put you in touch with brokers, whenever I mention a slightly obscure share in the *Daily Mail*, I am still liable to get calls and letters from people saying their bank cannot find it. That suggests banks may still have some way to go before they are really useful for penny share punters.

But if you make up your own mind about what you want to buy, and give your bank clear instructions, there is a chance. The one big feature in their favour is that, while they may not be brilliant at share trading, the High Street banks are substantial houses of standing. They may get muddled, but they will not run off with your money.

Building Societies

Similar observations apply to building societies. Some are nowhere near share dealing, of course. Others actually own stockbrokers. Where they offer share dealing facilities, you can expect integrity rather than expertise. Once again, if they are convenient, and you know what you want and can give clear instructions, they might be worth trying.

Share Shops

Things may change, but experience suggests share shops are something of a non-starter, unless they are the front office of a local and experienced stockbroker. Several big names who have tried them have pulled out, and some of the others have been run by unsuitable characters.

The notion that unsophisticated investors should be encouraged to walk in off the street and spend hundreds of pounds on the advice of someone behind the counter is frightening – but immensely attractive to get-rich-quick spivs who try it every so often.

Before you go near a share shop, check who owns it. Make sure it is run by members of the Stock Exchange, or someone of impeccable reputation. Do not take any notice of membership of the Securities and Futures Association, or some other self-regulatory organisation, no matter how important it may seem. Membership of the right regulator might ensure that you are in line for compensation in certain circumstances if your deal goes wrong. But you never want that to happen. And the loopholes will be many in practice, though you may be told that there are none at all. The regulators have too large a task to police everything properly. Relying on them is foolish. Use your common sense.

It is too easy to be led astray by a good salesperson who has something to sell, and commission to earn from selling it to you. You would not buy a car without thinking carefully about it. In a share shop, you might be tempted to spend almost as much money on the spur of the moment on a share you really know little about. It is too easy to be deceived in the investment game.

Proper share shops may work for those who know what they are doing, and decide what they want before they go through the door – and stick to it. But shops are shops, out to profit by selling. Never buy anything in a share shop without asking for detailed information first. Then go home and think about it. The delay is unlikely to cost you anything, at worst a few pence on the share price. The extra comfort of knowing you have not bought in haste is well worth it when you could be spending several hundred pounds, or maybe even a few thousand. Be careful.

Discount Dealing

There are several widely-promoted cut-price or discount dealing services. As usual, you need to be careful. In particular, I would steer clear of most dealing services linked to newspapers.

The most obvious disadvantage of many of these services is that they are postal-based, and give no guarantee of when they will buy or sell for you. Most reserve the right to hold your order until they have enough orders to buy or sell the share you are concerned with. Then they deal. This allows them to cut the commission charge by bulk trading. Unfortunately, it means your order could wait for hours – days even – until it is done. You might get a better price, or you might get a very much poorer one. It is a bit of a lottery, and no good to the sensible investor. You might save a few pounds on commission, and lose a lot more on the share price. Silly – especially when there could be all sorts of delays in the post to make it worse.

FIVE

What Makes a Penny Share Winner?

✸

Pinning down what makes any share a winner is difficult enough – without entertaining the extra perils and problems of penny shares. If there were clearly defined rules, everyone would follow them, everyone would be shifting their cash into the same shares, and there would be no big winners for anyone. Differences of opinion and the weight of money are what makes shares rise or fall. The more money shunted into a share, the higher it rises. It is elementary. When there are more buyers than sellers, and the demand persists, would-be buyers keep bidding the price up until they persuade people to sell to them, or until they themselves lose interest. Until there are more sellers than buyers, the price carries on up.

It sounds almost daft to set it out that way. Everyone knows that. But it is still worth underlining, because it is so easy to get tangled up in the intricacies of investment and to lose sight of the basics. Basic common sense is the greatest attribute any investor can have (after sheer good luck). Never lose sight of it. If something seems silly, if you cannot see how it makes sense, you are probably right. The odds are that it does not make sense, and that reality has gone out of the window for a while, taking the share price with it.

Your opinion, no matter how unfamiliar you may be with the inner workings of the investment world, could be the one which is right. It does not pay to be too dogmatic. We all get it wrong, perhaps too often to admit to ourselves sometimes. But in the stock market, your guess can be as good as the next investor's, though if they have more money than you, their guess might prevail for quite a while.

Money Rules, OK?

Share prices change in response to a vast range of different views from different investors, expressed by how they shift their money. For every buyer, there has to be a seller. For every one who thinks a particular share is going up, there has to be someone who thinks they have enough profit already, and ought to get out. When more people with more money think a particular share is good, it goes up. And vice versa.

If everyone saw the same opportunities at the same time, there would be no cheap shares, no bargains to buy. Nobody would be selling. There would be no market. There could be no winners because nobody would be prepared to risk losing a profit by selling a good thing.

Everyone a Winner

Do not get it wrong, however. Those who attack the system and suggest it thrives on cut-throat competition in which the winners can only prosper by taking from the losers are wrong. The Stock Exchange is not a zero-sum game. Winnings are not balanced out by losses. In the final analysis, share prices are determined by company profits and the expectation of profits. Because it is possible to build a thriving company from nothing, share prices can and do rise to reflect the creation of new wealth. When company profits are rising, share prices can rise happily to reflect the newly created prosperity, and to support and enhance it. When Tesco rises from 275p to 350p on the back of profits which leap through £700m, there has been a real gain for everyone. The only loss along the way has been the loss of a profit opportunity by those who sold Tesco shares at 275p. But they may have bought at 120p, and made profit enough along the way.

When some new high-tech computer software company rockets to market, and the shares double in the first six months of dealings, no-one loses. When Polly Peck leapt from a penny share to a £36 giant, it was based on dreams of creating a trading empire linking Northern Cyprus and Turkey with the rest of the world. No-one lost by that as it went up. Those who sell shares too quickly have missed a potential profit, nothing more. Each one of us, and the whole economy, benefits from a thriving company, with the hope that access to stock market funds will help further growth – for everyone.

Sadly, of course, there is another side of it. Polly Peck later plunged. The profits did not last, though the people who sold the shares while they were high know that their winnings were real enough.

What Goes Up, Stays Up. . . Sometimes

It is easy to say that what goes up must come down. It is a popular line among stock market cynics, commentators who want a simple way out. What goes up in the stock market may, indeed, come down. But anyone who invested in the leaders twenty years ago knows that though the shares have tumbled from time to time, there has been a real and lasting increase in value, and a very significant, important increase.

Never let me imply that there are no dangers in the stock market, that you do not run the risk of losing all of your money while a smarter investor will make a profit. The system can be cruel, and there are sharks galore in the water. The purpose of this book is to try to help you beat the sharks. There is nothing in the system to say that you cannot do it. You most certainly can.

Why Share Prices Rise

There is a host of reasons why investors rate some shares more highly than others. Dress it up how you may, prices ultimately rise because investors think profits earned by the underlying company will rise. Those profits, in turn, will be reflected in higher dividends to investors, and in a higher share price. The twists and turns are infinite, but in the end that is why more buyers than sellers pump money into a particular share – the anticipation of greater return. Do not lose sight of that.

Why Penny Shares are Different

Penny shares are influenced by the same rule. But while they are penny shares, the rules often appear different, because the prospect of good, steady profits is usually so distant. By the time that happy day arrives, the penny share punter will often be long gone, capital gain in pocket, seeking a new penny flyer.

Penny share opportunities fall into several different categories, but almost without exception, they have one important element in common. They occur in companies which are less secure than the average quoted company. The companies live nearer the edge than the others. They are either smaller, less mature, less dynamic, or are struggling. If the shares are worth buying, they are worth buying because things are going to change. The company will grow bigger, become better-established, develop a new lease of life, or it will recover and start to prosper.

Betting on such things is quite clearly a gamble. The fortunes of companies can change overnight, sometimes. They may not always change for the best. The biggest penny share winners are those which you can buy before the market realises things may change, before you yourself can possibly know for sure that they are going to change. You may make a killing by jumping aboard the gravy train after it has started rolling, but there is a chance that it will come off the rails even then. The old high reward / high risk ratio is inescapable. There is no such thing as a sure thing. What you need to do is to make sure the odds are in your favour, as far as possible.

Because of this, price earnings ratios and dividend yields count for much less in the penny share game. They hardly count at all in the beginning. What matters then is the great glorious blue sky beyond, where sometime, somehow, the penny share company will be transformed into a solid, secure giant, earning big profits and paying fat dividends. When that happens, the institutional investors, the City fat cats who make their investment decisions by the normal rules, will be queuing to buy because of the attractive price earnings ratio and the solid dividend yield. At first, though, that is a dim distant vision of what might be.

What sets a penny share moving is action – action of some sort which suggests that the company is going to start moving towards the day when there will be worthwhile profits. The action can take a variety of forms – new products, new management, a new deal – almost anything which opens up a fresh way forward. At the beginning, there may not be any regular profits of consequence, so the normal market concern with profits and dividends has nothing to focus on – just the hope that something will happen eventually to change that.

The change may be a long time coming. It may never happen. So instead of looking at penny shares by the more conventional measures of value, the prudent penny share player turns the order upside down, and puts asset strength at the top of the list of what really counts.

Assets, Assets, and More Assets

Usually you need assets, assets, and yet more assets, though the fashion for anything internet-related has changed that for a while The most important thing in a penny share is the asset value, what the company is really worth when it gets down to rock bottom. Because that is where the company could end up – at rock bottom. Penny share companies are not highly valued operations with stock market capitalisations running in to hundreds of millions of pounds. They will often be companies with a market value of twenty million pounds, frequently much less. If they were proven, established winners, bigger companies or acknowledged growth stocks with a bright future, they would not be penny shares. They would be nursed and coveted by an altogether better class of investor.

Because they are smaller, with less resources, penny share companies are more vulnerable. The small always get squeezed first if anything goes wrong, if the economy turns down, if a particular industry hits trouble, if a go-ahead director passes away or moves on. Often, their efforts are concentrated in one area of business. There is no comfortable spread to keep things ticking over if one part of the company hits trouble. Go back to the old cliché about banks and borrowing. If you owe £1,000 and cannot repay, the bank owns you. If you borrow £100 million and cannot repay, you might not own the bank, but you come close to it. The bank will want to help you, not crunch you. Big is better sometimes, even if that may not be what the penny share player is looking for.

One way or another, when it comes to penny shares there is no escaping the importance of asset value. It will determine how long a recovery stock can survive before the recovery starts coming through. Asset backing will attract a new management team before the old firm bows out and turns up its toes. If all else fails, asset backing is what might give shareholders a penny or two back should the liquidator step in to wind the company up. By that time, all hope may seem to be gone. But anyone who held shares in Rolls-Royce when it crashed in the Seventies will remember how the assets were sold for substantial sums, and eventually realised a small fortune. That allowed the liquidator to repay enough cash to make the shares big winners for those who bought just before the death.

Where to Find True Value

It would be nice to offer an easy way of finding out what really is the true asset value, to point to a ready indicator, something you can turn to in order to establish a company's worth. But such short cuts are hard to find. The *Investors Chronicle* gives an estimate of net asset value whenever it analyses company accounts. That can be useful. A few companies report their net asset value per share, and reference cards stored in most stockbroker's offices also give a figure. So does Jim Slater's publication *Company REFS*. But these calculations are generally based on a simple analysis of the balance sheet, and can prove misleading.

In a way, that is a bonus for penny share fans. If there was a fool-proof ready reference crib for penny shares and their asset backing, so many more market men would see the possibilities. Partly because you have to work a little, hunt around, there are opportunities which have been overlooked by the masses. Stockbroking analysts cannot punch up an instant electronic analysis of every penny share, complete with accurate asset value.

Ideally, what you want is a share you can buy for less than the value of its assets – in other words, if the company was wound up, and the parts sold, you would receive more from the liquidator than you paid for the shares. Like buying £1 notes for 50p, that is not too easy. But it can be done, especially when markets have been depressed for a while. The sensible way to start doing it is to get hold of a company's report and accounts, and plough through the balance sheet.

Do not lose heart if this sounds tough and technical. It is amazing what you can unravel with a little application. The balance sheet shows what the company owned, and what the company owed on the last day of the trading year. It is called a balance sheet because both sides, the assets and the liabilities, the pluses and the minuses, are meant to balance each other exactly.

Fixed Assets

Take a look first at the assets. Chase them through the notes at the back of the accounts to make sure you know what each category really means. There are fixed assets, things like land, factories, offices, and machinery. Look hard, and think about these.

Land values obviously vary enormously from place to place. A great tract of land housing an old engineering plant on the edge of a town in the North East of England may be worth less than a builders' yard in the heart of London. It could cost a fortune to tidy up the engineering site and use it for something else, even if there was a buyer with another use for it. A couple of acres in London with old offices and a few sheds to clear could be worth millions for redevelopment.

It is hard to know what is what just by looking at the balance sheet. Hunt through the report and accounts. Some companies list names and addresses of their subsidiary companies. There might be a clue there. Ask a local stockbroker if he knows anything which looks promising. Or buttonhole a director after a company meeting. Watch for comment that part of the business may be closed down, or operations are to be transferred from one factory to another. It could release a profitable site for something else. It is amazing how often that can be the saviour of a small company – or catches the eye of a well-informed bidder.

One bidder I know employed a man to look at every factory owned by a penny share company he was stalking. He asked local surveyors for valuations of each one. He was doing well until he was stopped by a security guard, who questioned why he was pacing the length of the car park wall. Another property whiz kid fell to his death from the roof of an office block he had wandered into, trying to check the floor area.

There are many others who take the business every bit as seriously, devote every bit as much attention to detail. They like to know what they are getting for their money, even if they only plan to buy a chunk of the shares and not the whole company. You may not be able to go to such lengths. But any effort should prove worthwhile.

Be sure to check when the properties were last valued. There should be a note in the accounts. Any values more than two years old might just be significantly understating the real worth. Be careful, though. In the early Nineties, values set in the late Eighties were almost certain to be overstated.

Often, though, if the values were set by the directors, they could have deliberately erred on the low side. After all, it might look unflattering if the company was seen to be making a low return from assets with a high value. And conservative directors often like to keep something up their sleeve, perhaps to avoid catching the eye of a predator, or to have ammunition to use to impress shareholders if there should be a bid.

Machinery is a more doubtful asset. Look for clues on how old it is. Some machines go on for tens of years, and retain their value. Others become outdated very quickly. The depreciation figure may help. High depreciation will suggest more modern machinery, losing value quickly. Lower depreciation might indicate older machines, perhaps worth more than their written value. But it can be a dangerous guessing game, and it is safest to assume that machines are worth less than in the balance sheet – maybe nothing – especially if profits are falling. Outdated, worthless machinery may explain why profits have been tumbling.

If there are investments listed among the fixed assets, hunt to see what they are. Obviously shares in a quoted company could have a ready value. More likely, investments will be a trade investment, a stake in a subsidiary partly owned by someone else. Look at the profit and loss account. That will show what has been taken off profits in the form of minority interests – profits due to the other shareholder in the trade investment. If the subsidiary is losing money, there will be an addition to the parent's profits under minority interests. Either way, that will give a crude indication of whether the investment is worth much – but only a crude indication.

Current Assets

Next come current assets – stocks, debtors, tax certificates, cash, and perhaps more investments. Stocks can be tricky. Who wants last year's Christmas annual, a Teenage Ninja Turtles T-shirt today, or spare wheels for a discontinued model? Treat them with scepticism, perhaps knock them out entirely. Debtors should be better, and represent the amount owed by other traders. Tax certificates are as good as cash, provided there are profits enough to pay tax on. Investments should be quoted and saleable, though they can rise and fall in value, and cash is precious to any company.

Liabilities

Current liabilities are the amount the company owns and must pay within twelve months; things like trade creditors (the normal bills incurred for materials and such), overdrafts, and perhaps the tax bill. Deduct current liabilities from current assets, and you get net current assets. The bigger, the better, though sometimes you will find the bills are too big and there are net current liabilities, which suggests the company is short of cash and may have to ask shareholders for more.

The usual balance sheet routine is to add net current assets to fixed assets (or take away net current liabilities). Then other liabilities are taken off. These will consist of loans which may have several years to run before repayment. Take them away, and what is left are the net assets – what there would be for shareholders if the business was sold off in pieces.

Asset Value Per Share

The next section shows how these assets are treated in the company's capital structure. The amount of paid up share capital takes the Ordinary shares at their nominal, or par value. Then there will be reserves, which come from the cash left over through the years after paying tax and dividends. Add reserves to share capital, and you have shareholders' funds.

It is worth watching just how great shareholders' funds are in relation to the amount of borrowing. The higher borrowing levels go – often referred to as the gearing – the greater the dangers. It varies from company to company, and industry to industry, but if borrowings are as great as shareholders funds – a one to one ratio – watch out. Anything above a 50% borrowing ratio is uncomfortable.

If you can get hold of it, there is now an excellent guide to gearing and a whole lot else, in *Company REFS*. This is updated regularly, but is expensive for small investors. Try to find a copy in your public library or a business library. Or ask your broker if he has it, and can send you the sheet on the company you are investigating.

The real purpose of our balance sheet exercise is to ferret out the asset value. It is handiest when translated into net asset value per share. To do that, simply take the shareholders' funds, and divide them between the number of Ordinary shares in issue. If you have shareholders' funds of £100,000, and 50,000 shares in issue, the net asset value is £2 a share.

Do not forget, though, that the figure you have taken from the balance sheet may not be what it appears to be. All of those adjustments we have suggested

– perhaps upgrading the worth of the land because of development potential, downgrading because of an office slump in London, knocking a lot off the value of stocks, restating the worth of the trade investment – may give you a rather different picture. It should be a more accurate one.

Asset Extras

There are a few asset extras to keep in mind. These days, a conservative accountant or analyst may knock goodwill out of the balance sheet entirely. Goodwill normally arises when one company buys another, and pays more than asset value. The difference between asset value and purchase price is put down to goodwill, and that goodwill may be knocked off profits as they are earned over the next few years. Accounting wrangles over this go on forever, and take us into the realms of creative accounting.

What concerns penny punters more is that goodwill may have a positive value. It arises in the most literal sense. Brand names, for example, are usually in a company's books for a nominal sum. People are familiar with the brand, and like it. Advertising it is easy. That can mean it carries enormous and very valuable goodwill.

The name Bush Radio changed hands for a small fortune, just so a couple of enterprising lads could stick it on TVs and such imported from the Far East. They floated the company, and saw it taken over for a tidy sum. The name alone made an enormous difference to the value, because customers were ready to buy Bush products. It had a good reputation from a different era.

When it comes to asset value, then, do not forget brand names or the value of an old-established business. It may not be measurable in plain pounds and pence, but it can be a very big plus.

Or a minus. Robert Maxwell valued the Mirror newspaper titles at nearly £600m when he floated the company, an absurd overvaluation. Some now account for brand names as a real tangible value. Look carefully. It may make sense – but not always.

Overseas subsidiaries are another source of hidden assets. They can sometimes be in the books for very little. Fobel, a penny share company which blazed to the heights in the early Eighties only to topple again, did well for investors a second time around. It had a small stake in a North American door company bought for a tiny sum. When the door company went public, Fobel's holding was valued at millions of pounds.

Pension funds, too, have become a valuable source of loot. The Inland Revenue has been making life more difficult, but companies which have cut their workforce sharply in recent years often find that they are left with a pension fund stuffed with goodies, vastly overfunded. The strength of the stock market in the Eighties meant that investments which were bought to provide income in future years scored massive capital growth, far beyond expectations. Big companies have released tens of millions of pounds back into the business, cutting their own pension payments, reducing the amount put in by present workers, and still finding lots left over. One of the great bonuses for Sir Owen Green and his BTR giant when they took over Dunlop was the fortune which could be taken out of the pension fund. Many a smaller bid has quietly turned on the extra cash the raider knew he could squeeze from the fund.

Watch out for a business which has laid off a lot of workers in the past few years. The real values are hard to track down. Once again, a quiet word with the finance director at a company meeting might yield a clue or two.

Thanks again to Maxwell, it has become a tricky subject. Do not be frightened off by the Max factor. There can be a perfectly honourable bonus for companies in retrieving pension surpluses.

Property Companies

Some years back, property investment companies were the fat asset plums. They would be sitting on prime properties, drawing rents, and watching their value grow steadily. General practice was to revalue the assets in the balance sheet on a conservative basis. And the shares often sold at 30% or 40% below real worth.

That changed as traditional companies were taken over. Other companies came on the scene, financing new developments and trading them out for a profit. Many later got caught with massive borrowings and uncompleted and unsold developments. Interest charges far outstripped the income from rents, and it became impossible to make profits by selling developments. Shares entered the Nineties selling at 30%-40% below what was claimed to be their real worth once again. Realistically, many had no chance of selling assets for book value, and were struggling for survival. Come the late Nineties, after a happier spell, question marks began to rise again. So be careful. Stay clear of property companies unless you can approach them with the aid of expert advice. Property is very much a specialist area.

How Much Asset Backing?

As we entered the new century, the internet fashion had so caught the imagination of punters and promoters alike that the hunt for value had been overtaken by a rush for almost anything which was not actually falling apart. Company promoters who once hesitated at paying £100,000 over real worth for control of a company began to pay a £500,000 premium, happy to do it. Trying to suggest that the penny punter should stick to shares which boasted an asset value equal to the share price was futile. If such gems existed, there was good reason why no-one had snapped them up.

In tearaway markets, asset guide-lines become almost meaningless. In the internet excitement, the dream of countless millions somewhere in cyberspace has prompted a rush into shares which sell at many times asset value. Without wishing to join the gloom merchants who predict it will end in tears, you should look very hard before paying more than three times asset value for an otherwise empty cash shell.

From time to time, though, there are real asset bargains about. Hunt them out. They are easier to find – but when you think you have spotted them, check liquidity first. It is no good finding a vast store of assets which cannot be translated into cash in a company which might go bust because it cannot meet the day-to-day bills. Look for cash in the balance sheet, low borrowings, and a line of operation which keeps a good flow of cash coming in. Cash flow is crucial, with more and more investors realising that it does matter.

Cash flow counts for survival, alongside saleable assets at the top of any enterprising new management team's hit list, all else being equal. In the Eighties, my pal with the valuer visiting factories in his car was not playing around. He was selecting his target, trying to ensure that when he did come to market, he had the most solid backing he could find. He wanted a small company with big assets. These days, he might fancy the assets, but he will want to be certain that he can repay any borrowings, or at least ensure that the bank will support him without calling in overdrafts. He will be looking for assets which produce income. And he will want to raise capital by selling assets, so he can then pump it in a business which generates cash.

Not everyone prepares carefully. In the mid-Eighties, one set of big money winners bought into a company at a few minutes' notice. They had just taken one clapped-out business, multiplied the share price eight-fold with a quick series of sharp acquisitions, and sold out within two years of the first deal. They had made many millions each, and wanted to try again.

Second time around, they were so confident that their starting price and the asset backing hardly mattered. The moment the City saw their names on a share stake, the new vehicle trebled, before they had lifted a finger.

Penny share punters know about such things. They dream of them. Sadly, my super-confident winners found they had few tangible assets, and had bought a few indifferent businesses for their new shell too quickly. The share rise was halted by the recession, and no-one wanted to take their paper – they had no decent assets to sell to raise cash, so they could not do more deals. The duds they had bought failed to produce the profits they expected, so the shares tumbled. A little while later, the company was limping along, the original promoters had jumped ship, and the shares were one tenth of their previous price. Asset strength and proper research does count after all.

The Conventional Tools

Once you understand where you are with penny share asset values, you can turn to the conventional tools most employ as measures of investment worth – the price earnings ratio and the dividend yield. The City uses them all of the time. At one stage you heard the UK average price earnings ratio compared with America. Then our shares, on a hefty 20-times earnings, were suddenly paraded as cheap by comparison with Japanese companies trading on 200-times earnings. Japanese shares were different, for a while. In the late Nineties, they were trading on perhaps 15-times earnings after a long, deep stock market slide. The big league averages can change. And in 2000, of course, there were many companies trading with pe ratios of several hundred – even a few thousand.

Price Earnings Ratios

The key way of translating profits into investment jargon is through the price earnings ratio, the most widely used piece of investment shorthand for comparing the profits of one company with those of another.

It is variously called the 'price earnings ratio', 'p/e ratio', the 'pe', x year's earnings', or 'x times earnings'. It tells you how many years it would take a company to earn profits enough to equal its stock market value.

The profits which matter are those struck after paying tax and paying dividends due on any Preference capital – in other words, the net profits attributable to Ordinary shareholders. These are the profits which could in theory be paid out in dividends if the company chose to. We came across them earlier when we looked at profit statements and company accounts. Often they are translated into earnings per share, or eps, or simply, earnings.

This is done by dividing profits after tax and Preference dividends into the number of Ordinary shares in issue. Say our company has one million £1 shares in issue, and makes profits after tax of £500,000. That company has earned profits of 50p for every share – or has earnings per share of 50p. If the share price is 450p, it would take nine years for the company to make profits enough to equal the share price, assuming profits did not change. Divide the earnings per share into the share price, and you arrive at the price earnings ratio. So shares selling at 450p are on a price earnings ratio of nine if the company has earnings per share of 50p.

If you find this a little difficult to work out from published information, do not worry. Ask. Anyone who deals in shares should have it at their fingertips. And it is published daily with the share price list in several papers.

It does not matter if you cannot work it out yourself. But it is important to be able to use it, because it gives a quick clue to the relative rating of the shares. Broadly speaking, a high price earnings ratio means the market is expecting fast profit growth, and a low one means that there may be problems.

Look at other companies in the same line of business. If their price earnings ratio is significantly different, find out why. Either the company you are looking at is out of line, and may be dear or cheap. Or there is a good reason for the difference. Do not get too excited. In most cases, there will be an obvious explanation for any variation, and it will be widely understood. You do not stumble on too many obvious mistakes in these markets. The professionals comb the lists of p/e ratios too carefully.

Dividend Yields

In the roaring bull markets of the Nineties, prices were increasingly p/e driven. Less attention was paid to dividends and dividend yields. In harder times, however, these are what count. Insurance companies and pension funds, the big investors who really move the market, buy shares for a steady stream of rising income to match the commitments they have to policy holders and pensioners. Capital gains are a massive bonus, but dividends are vital.

Dividends – the amount companies pay shareholders out of each year's profits – matter particularly to investors on fixed incomes, or nearing retirement. And they are growing more important now so many people have Personal Equity Plans and can use them to take dividends free of tax. Many investors buy shares for the income they will produce, regardless of capital gain. That may not concern the penny share punter directly, but it is worth keeping in mind because it will attract other investors, who will buy the shares and provide the capital growth that penny players are hunting.

The dividend yield shows the percentage return you get each year by buying shares at the current price – the same sort of thing as the 7% interest on your building society account. If you get £10 a year in dividend from investing £100, the yield is 10%. Buy 200 shares at £2 each, get a dividend of 10p a year on each share, and the yield is 5%. Calculate this by taking the total dividend (10p multiplied by 200 equals £20), dividing this by the total cost (200 times £2 is £400) and expressing it as a percentage – 5%.

As before, you need not worry about working it out yourself. Tax complications – the business of whether the payment is calculated net of tax or gross – means the detail is quite complicated. Do not bother yourself. Any investment adviser will tell you, and many papers print yields each day in their share tables.

As share prices rise, so dividend yields fall, because you are paying more for the right to the same amount of dividend. As prices fall, so dividend yields rise. Most companies like to pay a higher dividend each year, if they can, so as time goes by, your effective dividend yield rises when set against your original purchase price.

A low yield tends to suggest investors expect a good rate of profits growth, leading to higher dividends in future. And a high yield indicates that the market fears there will be no growth, or even a reduced dividend. Or sometimes a low yield indicates that a payment has just been cut. Like most investment rules, even this simple notion can be turned on its head.

Like the price earnings ratio, the dividend yield gives a pointer to how a share is rated. Compare the yield to those on companies in the same sort of business. Always remember, though, to check exactly what you are looking at. Dividend yields and price earnings ratios in most newspapers are based on the last reported dividend and profits. This year's profits and dividends could be different. Sometimes the figures are based on a forecast from the company. A historic price earnings ratio of 15, say, can be very different to a prospective price earnings ratio of 15, calculated on a forecast by the company of sharply higher profits ahead.

The Mystery Share Movers

Asset values, price earnings ratios, and dividend yields are all capable of some sort of independent confirmation. You can have a reasonable idea of what they are about. But when you play the share game, a host of other factors comes into play, shunting prices up and down. The moves may appear a complete mystery. But that is only because you do not have the full picture. You never will. After all, how could you expect to discover that a market-maker cut his prices to try to get rid of several thousand shares because his firm's resident economist took a gloomy view of next winter's trade figures – and the economist took that line because he had dinner with a chum in Whitehall who was feeling under the weather at the time?

The lines of communication can grow so long and so convoluted that they appear to defy all logic. But they still make prices move. Big investors do buy and sell large lines of shares for reasons which have absolutely nothing to do with the intrinsic merit of those shares. It may reflect an unforeseen situation in the investment house itself. Professional share gamblers do take very large positions, sometimes for quite the wrong reasons. They make mistakes like all of us. Fun and games in the Far East virtually bust the blue-blooded Barings merchant bank. Sometimes the mistakes are almost unbelievably foolish. It is not too often that someone trades shares because they have the company name wrong. But even that happens. Stupidity can – and does – move prices.

You could be a genius. You could have spotted a company whose profits were poised to leap, and you could still lose money because some apparently unrelated event means other people are selling. It happens. I well remember how keenly I told *Daily Mail* readers to buy shares in Alan Sugar's electronics company Amstrad in the mid-Eighties. Twice I tipped them. Nothing happened. They perked up, and drifted back. Because I operate a stop-loss system to advise readers when they should sell shares (more of that later), I told everyone to get out with a loss of a few pence per share. Within six months, the profits I had dreamt of at Amstrad had come true. The shares soared six – seven – eight-fold. I had been absolutely right, sort of. But my investment advice – so nearly right – was completely wrong. I never did discover why the shares dipped, and triggered my sell signal.

The lesson is worth emphasising. No matter how right you may be on some parts of the equation, as an investor, you are wrong unless others agree, and the weight of their buying pushes the price up – for whatever reason. You can be too smart for your own good.

SIX

The Ideal Penny Share – and Where to Find It

✸

What makes the ideal penny share? So far, we have managed to sketch a basic outline. Hopefully, it will have a hefty asset backing, and hold the promise of some kind of action sooner or later. Fundamentals like the price earnings ratio and dividend yield may not matter too much, and it will probably not be a property company. What other clues are there in hunting the ideal penny share?

A Modest Market Value

For starters, it will almost certainly have a modest market value. The whole company will probably be worth less than £20 million, as measured by the price of the shares. Market capitalisation is the City term, or 'market cap' in dealerspeak. Multiply the number of shares in issue by their price, and you have it. Newspaper price tables show the market capitalisation of companies whose price they carry, though several only do it on Monday or Saturday. Very handy, so long as the shares you want to know about are listed there. Quite often, they will not be, because they are too small.

Merely finding such essential information is a problem for the private investor – and for many others. *Company REFS* carries it. One of the easiest routes is to ask your broker – if you have one – to look for you on his terminal. Most can search the internet or have access to a service provided by a company called Hemmington Scott. Or they can get to Datastream, a computer-backed service which carries a mass of information about most quoted companies.

From time to time, I programme Datastream to hunt all public companies valued at £100 million or less. There are usually too many to cope with in the normal fashion. The same answer is liable to crop up at £20 million. Usually, I end up going for companies valued at £5 million or less. Frequently, there are 300 or more. There always seem to be at least 200. So do not let anyone tell you the little companies are gone, and they have all been snapped up. They are there, if only you can find them.

Why are companies worth under £20 million the best? Simple. They are the most affordable, not just to private shareholders, but also to ambitious new managers. Look at the lists of top performing shares each year. The majority are smaller companies which have been picked up, shaken, turned inside out and rebuilt by a new team at the top. In helping other shareholders, they have helped themselves. That is what makes many share winners – a keenly motivated team, out to build a thriving business and make a fortune for themselves in the process.

Understandably, it is a management approach which makes real sense – self-help. Though they might run a giant empire, many big company directors have not been able to get themselves a sufficiently large slice of the action in the early days. When they have succeeded in driving the company forward, they have earned generous rewards, but the big shareholders have done much better. Had the managers started in a shell company, and achieved similar growth, they would have made themselves much more money. They would have held 20% or 30% of the company, from the beginning. Instead of asking shareholders for share options which might reward their effort with a few million pounds if they continue to get it right, and risking controversy over fat cat pay bonuses, they would have been worth tens of millions as major shareholders.

Anyone who starts out, though, with a relatively large piece of a small company has to find the cash to buy in at the beginning, no matter how fast he is going to make it grow. So the smaller the starting company, the better.

Greg Hutchings, who followed in the footsteps of his mentor, Lord Hanson, by building Tomkins into a classic, fast-growing, acquisitive engineering conglomerate, multiplied the value of the original share stake more than twenty-fold in the first four years. He borrowed heavily to buy his way in, and later paid off his borrowings by selling a small number of shares at a hefty profit. Hutchings won, and so did shareholders who had backed him from the beginning, though share price growth had ground almost to a halt by the mid-Nineties. Come 2000, he was forced to reshape the whole company.

Perhaps the most successful of more recent shell company operators has been former stockbroking analyst Luke Johnson, son of writer Paul Johnson. He has made a fortune building companies like Pizza Express, bringing them to market in a smaller operator where he had a sizeable share stake, and then watching them grow. He did a highly profitable job injecting Utility Cable, which laid cables for the TV companies, into an investment trust shell. After a while, the shares slipped as profits proved disappointing. But for Johnson fans who sold sensibly (see the crucial Chapter Nine), it was a triumph. Now whenever he moves into a small company – restaurants group Belgo is among his recent flyers – the price rises sharply. Usually, it pays off.

Many a high flyer starts in hock, mortgaged to the hilt. In good times, bright boys can get bright backers, pushing money at them. But it costs. So unless they can find a relatively modestly valued company to work on, they will be left with too small a stake as the saga unfolds.

That is what makes companies with a market value of under £20 million so attractive. Even securing a worthwhile piece of a £10 million company imposes a massive burden on a potential management ace. So the smaller the shell, the better.

It is plain, too, to see that it is easier to build more rapidly from a small base. As Jim Slater, in his book *The Zulu Principle,* remarks, "Elephants don't gallop". It takes a couple of shrewd deals to turn a £2 million company into a £10 million company. A few more to take it to £50 million, then £100 million, multiplying the original value 50 times. Because of the extra shares issued along the way, the original share price might not have risen 50-fold. But it could well have multiplied ten times over.

Start, though, with a £500 million company, and you might push the value to £2,000 million with two or three well-judged deals. A formidable achievement, which could well see the share price multiply two, or three times. But making the next few leaps will take enormous effort. Getting to £5,000 million might be possible. It might take the shares up a further two or three times. Building a business from £500 million to £5,000 million would be remarkable. But it is unlikely to be rewarded by a share price appreciation to match that accorded the dealer who makes the much easier move from £2 million to £100 million – and can make it in a much shorter time.

Share Stakes

Penny share winners, then, are most likely among companies with a market value under £20 million. Early in 1992, management whiz kid Alan Bowkett bought into Berisford International, which had then sold British Sugar, and was effectively an £80m shell. So the rule is not inflexible. But it will serve you well. There is no shortage of companies which qualify. Once you have found them, check who owns them.

Like so many investment tips, those on share stakes can be turned upside down to suit the occasion. What you need is either a company where nobody holds any sizeable stake – or one with a few big holders. It depends on attitudes.

If there are no significant large investors, a new team may be able to gain a position of influence relatively easily. They can start by accumulating shares for themselves quietly. Anyone can tuck away 2.9% of a company without coming into the open. Only holders of more than 3% – or members of the board – have to declare their interest in public. Strictly speaking, any group acting together in what the City calls a concert party has to own up when the total share tops 3%. In practice, this line gets fuzzy. The chaps may simply be acting together, each buying the same shares because each one thinks he has spotted a good investment. Two or three of them, maybe more, could each pick up 2.9% without declaring their interest. And if, by chance, they should all realise that their interests coincide, they could discover that they have 15% or 20% of the company between them. How convenient.

Life's little coincidences often happen, unnoticed, around the edges of the rules. Sometimes shares get parked. Investment dealers who look after other people's money will buy large numbers of shares in one company, parcelling them out to clients. When the action starts, and a suitable team comes looking for shares enough to take control of the company, all of the investment adviser's clients may be persuaded to sell. There might be several hundred of them, some with just a few thousand shares. They will have taken a nice profit along the way, and will probably keep a few more shares for the ride.

No rules will have been broken, and everyone will do nicely out of this happy chance. Except, perhaps, the former directors, who will find new men knocking on their door, inviting them to leave. If the old board members have any sense, they will do a quiet deal for fat golden handshakes or consultancy fees, and tuck away a few shares. If they choose to fight, they may discover a surprisingly large proportion of their shareholders know the new boys, and act as a sort of fan club, ready to back whatever the new boys suggest.

Alternatively, there are attractions in finding a company where the established management has a controlling stake, and is ready to cash in and sell out. There are smaller companies still dominated by the original family who built the business and brought it to market. Through the years, they have lost their energies, and the business may have drifted, battered by the recession. Shareholdings may have been dispersed, spread wide among the family as successive generations have married and taken a few shares with them. The surnames may have changed, and the extent of the controlling stake may not be visible from scanning the list of directors.

It may still exist, however. And though you can be sure that all controlling investors in such companies will have been approached many times over the years, there are always some who reach the end of the road eventually. The right offer from the right people at the right time is always liable to unlock control.

What the private investor has to do is decide just when that might happen. It is not easy. Obviously the age of the controlling directors is important. Some ease out as they approach retirement, or fall ill. Others cling on until they die, business their main reason for living. Others battle on for years, then give up when the competition gets too tough. Other simply decide it is time to buy that boat and sail around the Mediterranean. All the individual investor can do is to keep an ear open for gossip. Or perhaps go to the company meeting, and weigh up the chances, face to face with the directors.

It does not always work that way. Sometimes newcomers do surface for all to see with a 3% plus stake, or more. Rarely will this happen by accident. The players all know the value of declaring a stake in a public company. It will be put out in the open for a variety of reasons.

Professionals call it 'putting the company in play'. Usually the idea is to attract speculators into the shares, so that a higher percentage of the stock is waiting for a bid, ready to accept when it comes. Sometimes, the idea is partly to unsettle the old team, to persuade them to pep things up, and the new boys are simply putting on a gentle display of strength. Now and then, it may mean that the old board has been watching the share register carefully, uncovered a build-up of shares under nominee names, and has chosen to force it out into the open.

Alternatively, the stakeholder may be gently advertising his shares for sale, ready to pass on to someone who may be looking for such a company. Or he may think other undisclosed predators are lurking, and might join in. At times, the stake will simply be declared for everyone to see, hoping the market will consider it the prelude to action, and so bump the share price up. Then the stakeholder can sell, take a profit, and walk away. Once again, then, there are no absolute, copper-bottomed certainties for penny share punters, just a variety of options to weigh. But being aware of them will give you an edge on the other fellow, who may not have thought about them at all. Action of any sort is always a good sign.

Tracking share stakes is not too difficult, given a little dedication. The accumulation of 3% or more, changes to that stake, or changes in a director's holding, must be declared to the Stock Exchange within two working days of the change. Those changes appear on the electronic screens which most brokers and advisers have. Unfortunately, the information may not stay there for long, and could be wiped off before many spot it.

The financial press does monitor share stakes, but even the *Financial Times* is not a completely reliable source for all of them. They are published in the *Stock Exchange Weekly Official Intelligence*, which you will find in many larger libraries. And they appear eventually on the various printed reference services which cover quoted companies. There are a couple of services which publish lists of directors' share dealings, but they are rather pricey for private investors. The *Financial Times* prints a useful list of directors' deals on Saturdays.

Such deals are additionally helpful, of course, as a means of following just how directors – the ultimate insiders – view the fortunes of their own companies. Some buy or sell for perfectly innocent reasons, unconnected with the progress of their companies. But that is not always so. Cynics will make their own judgement on what determines how directors trade. But keeping track of the moves can yield valuable insight into what lies ahead.

The Message in the Share Price

Share trading by the board may not always move the price, but changes in the price can give some of the most valuable clues in picking a winner. Shares can send out their own messages, loud and clear, if you are ready to hear. There is no great mystery in it. It comes back to the time-honoured business of insider trading.

Somebody always knows what is going on. Somebody always deals. It is pointless arguing over definitions and degrees of naughtiness. Whenever a predator spots a suitable target, he has to start buying at some stage. And there is nothing wrong with it. Who can say exactly when the emphasis shifts to something questionable and beyond the legitimate accumulation of shares ahead of a public move to take control? Is it perhaps with the purchase of a few shares by his advisers, or friends who know what is afoot? One of the best-known corporate financiers in the City has a firm rule for his clients in a bid – if they do not have a share stake in the target company before they start, they will not win. Of course, as soon as it becomes apparent to the outside world that his client has a share stake, the plan is undone. So the stake has to be built by stealth, or at speed. That is standard practice in the real world, how it really happens, never mind the official line.

Whatever, the indisputable rule is that the share price tells the story. But often, no-one realises what it is saying. Reading the message is not always easy, but sometimes it leaps out at you.

The first thing is to watch prices, day in, day out. For most people, that means checking newspaper lists, even though they are unreliable. Every one, from the *Financial Times* down, gets prices wrong, sometimes quite frequently. It happens in all newspapers. Changes are marked the wrong way, or go unreported for several days. It is no good getting angry with the journalists. A couple of times, we have run the same share price table in the *Daily Mail* on successive days. Other newspapers have done the same. It might appear daft, but no matter what safeguards are built in to modern computer systems, it still seems someone can press the wrong buttons and make everyone look silly. So far, the perfect system has not reached the City pages.

The internet has made an amazing difference. Now you can follow prices pretty closely. There are all sorts of on-line services which allow you to track prices. If you want real-time prices so you can watch them as they change, you will need to pay extra – perhaps £10 a month, maybe more on certain systems. Many others, though, will offer free access to prices with a fifteen- or twenty-minute delay. I list some of them later in the book. By the time you read this, there will probably be others, and there may well be free real-time prices you can access. The system is changing quickly.

Some more costly systems will allow you to access the same information as you see on ICV in brokers' offices. There the day's opening price is in green. Red means a fall, blue a rise. If you are concentrating in a share, you can often detect a pattern. If you do not see the colours, you can still track it by watching carefully. There are shares which move up a few pence, fall a touch, then rise again. The price falls 2p, and picks up 2p. The sellers come in again, three, maybe four deals. Then the buyers reappear, taking the price up, but perhaps not to the previous level. Gradually you realise that there may be someone there, picking up shares quietly on each setback. That is the professional way, quietly, not forcing the price up. At the close, it may be down a touch. But by watching carefully, you may be happy to conclude there is buying support, somebody seems to know something. There may be more sellers than buyers, but instead of the price getting pushed down and down, someone has the nerve to accumulate stock.

It may not mean anything. The pattern may simply be chance. But if you do have regular access to a screen, you can sometimes see it happening, day after day. Then you really can feel reasonably secure, even though it may take months to be confirmed.

Sometimes it happens after a share has had a sharp rise. A flurry of sellers comes in, taking profits. The price is marked down quite sharply because the market-makers know what is happening. They know the selling brokers were buying a few days before. They have a rough idea of how many shares those brokers may have to sell – though they can never be sure, and can never know that the shares have not gone out through a different door, sold to another market-maker. Watch, though, and sometimes the screen will show a steady stream of blue moves coming in after a fall. Someone is quietly picking up a holding, taking out the short-term profit takers, and is ready to sit a little longer and wait for a bigger move up.

The variations are infinite. Often, they will be indecipherable, apparently random. But you can learn to read them. They do carry a strong signal, sometimes with obvious implications. Especially if you watch the same prices over an extended period, be it weeks, months, or years.

Certain shares do develop a pattern. Some stocks always run up ahead of good profit news, and fall most of the way down again, no matter how good the figures. Others – Lonrho used to be a prime example before profits started falling apart – start to improve several weeks ahead of a dividend payment. High income investors were buying for the right to the large dividend cheque.

Simplest to spot are shares which deviate from the norm – those which rise or hold steady when the market is falling apart, or which fall in the middle of a boom. Someone always knows something. Someone always deals.

There are shares which slump on news of poor profits, find a level, then begin to creep up again. Perhaps some predator is building a stake. There are shares which scarcely stir for weeks on end, then begin to edge ahead. Someone may be building a stake. There are shares which report terrible figures, but hardly budge. Someone may be building a stake. And there are shares which leap dramatically, without explanation. Someone may have built a stake, and may be going to pounce tomorrow.

It happens, believe me. Forget pious statements from the Stock Exchange, declarations of intent that all shareholders should be treated equally, all given the same information at the same time. It does not work that way. The rules may get tighter, and the Stock Exchange may probe more suspicious price moves. It has, in fact, taken a useful step forward by forcing companies to issue statements more often after a big share move, threatening to suspend the shares if the company does not obey. That is fine. But if you want to pick winning shares, you want the ones with action ahead. And, short of clear inside information which could land you in prison if you use it, there is no better clue to what is going to happen than to study how the price behaves.

In the quieter times, it can be instructive simply to get to a screen, and flick through page by page, noting where there is action. In smaller companies especially, there may be no marks of business at all. Others will have three or four changes against them. They may not generate any real change in price. Sometimes there will have been a little flurry because profits have been announced. Sometimes, though, there will be no apparent reason for the interest. Those are the stocks worth checking. Something may be afoot. Traders are not acting for no reason.

The Charts

Perhaps the handiest way of spotting when the share price gives the game away is to follow the charts. There is a whole industry built around charting the course of share prices, with great gurus employed to pronounce on every flip of a penny piece, services selling wonderfully drawn books of charts, and computer software which will track your rocket to the moon. There are books to tell you what the terms mean – and wonderful terms they are, too. *Charters on Charting* by David Charters is a good starting point. Soon you can become familiar with the world of double bottoms, heads and shoulders, spear points, flags and goodness knows what else.

Some investors swear by them, believe in nothing else. They insist on following a pattern of blobs, dots, or squares on a page, refusing to worry whether company profits are leaping or plunging. For them it is all in the charts.

It is easy to poke fun, but charts can have their uses, even for the most sceptical investor. Perhaps their greatest attribute is that they tend to throw up insider dealing clues more clearly than most other systems.

Chartists may blob the closing price each day on a vertical scale, with the time period on the horizontal. They may draw a vertical line covering the high and low trading range for the day. They may compile a point and figure chart, with a vertical row of crosses for each worthwhile gain, and a nought for each fall, making a new column with each change of direction.

However they do it, the marks tend to cluster around a particular level, as shares hover in a limited range. That happens to most shares, most of the time. The important event is when the price begins to move away from that cluster, up or down. Something is happening. Chartists draw their own projections to arrive at all manner of conclusions from unusual moves. Show half a dozen the same chart, and they may arrive at six different conclusions as to what will happen next. You can believe them, or not, as you choose. But for the penny share punter, on the alert for action, what matters is that something is afoot. The charts show up most clearly when a share has begun to behave unusually. And that is what you want to spot.

When that happens, abandon ideas of what the chartists think the price will do, and begin asking around, concentrating on gossip about your chosen company. It might be a false alarm, but there might be a message in the price. If someone has bought sufficient shares to shake the price out of a long-established trading range, they might have a very good reason for doing it. Someone might be closing in on the company. Equally, of course, if the price falls lower than usual, there might be unexpected bad news to come. Write that one off your list of prospective purchases for the time being.

The Highs and Lows

In similar fashion, it pays to watch highs and lows. Many tables show the highest price and the lowest price a share has touched in the year. A new high, or a new low, and you should wake up and start paying attention. If you have watched the charts, of course, you will already know, and may be aware of how the price has been behaving for rather more than the past year. The longer it was confined to the range it has moved out of, the more important the move.

High and low levels are a cruder guide, but can be especially useful if you want to keep an eye on more shares than you can follow on charts. The simplest guide comes in the *Financial Times*. Its prices page lists new highs and lows each day. Unfortunately, on busy days, individual shares are not always named. The most interesting are those breaking new boundaries on days when they needed a special reason to move, and were not just carried away with the overall momentum of the market.

Newspapers

Already I have made it clear that there is much to be gleaned from the financial press. The City pages are essential regular reading for any share punter in my view – but that is where I earn my living. Financial journalists may make mistakes, may sometimes be dreadfully lacking in judgement, and may sometimes be far less experienced and informed than you might think. But they offer one very important advantage – they are independent.

Most financial journalists are honest and well-intentioned. Like anyone, they have their favourites, and their pet hates. But all they are trying to sell you is their newspaper. In approaching 40 years, I have heard a continual rumble suggesting that City journalists buy shares, write them up, and sell to make a killing. Or that they are tipped off by all sorts of people and have the advantage of insider information to use to line their own pockets.

Most of that is nonsense. There have been journalists who cheat. There may still be some. But they are few and far between. Perhaps the biggest danger is journalists who have never actually bought or sold a share, and who still think they are qualified to tell others how to do it. These days, it is harder than ever to get real inside information. It does happen. But no journalist would dare use it to anything but the advantage of the readers.

For better or worse, the financial press is a valuable source of relatively unbiased information. Use it. Pay close attention to stock market reports. They have the kind of gossip which passes over City lunch tables. Some of it is wildly inaccurate – but much of it has a good foundation in truth. Just because some of the things City pages predict do not happen, it is unwise to assume that they were never intended to happen. Plans change – and company directors are not always truthful. They do sometimes say no when the answer should be yes. And it does not always matter whether the rumours are sheer bunkum or not. If they move the price, you want to know about them.

Obviously there is no substitute for the *Financial Times*. It lacks share tipsters, outside the Saturday pages and the occasional efforts of the Lex column, the back page piece of punditry which varies in quality with the individuals who write it. But the *Financial Times* has the broadest coverage of all. It is not complete, but there is nothing better.

Especially useful to penny share punters is the Saturday edition. In addition to the normal price table, it carries details of dealings done in the preceding week in all securities outside the daily *FT* list. That is the most readily available source of prices for smaller mining stocks traded on overseas exchanges, and dealings in mineral exploration companies.

Obviously the resources of other City pages cannot match the *Financial Times*. But the *Mail* City section has a good reputation for spotting unusual moves, picking up the gossip, and for strong opinions.

Derek Pain, the veteran stock market reporter on the *Independent*, is particularly useful in providing information about small companies. Other newspapers, especially the Sundays, carry share tips. Beware those which scatter unresearched snippets, though they are a useful starting point for investigation. They tend to trumpet their successes, forget the losers, and all too rarely make any mention of when to take profits. If you follow a regular column, be careful if it uses a pen name rather than the name of an individual journalist. Such columns vary in quality with the writers, and journalists move from paper to paper frequently. If you find one you like, follow the name, not the column.

Magazines

No financial magazine compares with the *Investors Chronicle*, a weekly which is essential to any half-serious investor. It carries a first-class mixture of investment features, tips, and analysis. The regular examination of company accounts is an unrivalled source of useful facts – including intelligent estimates of asset value – and the comment on company events is excellent for keeping in touch.

All of a sudden, though, in the year 2000, the *Investors Chronicle* faces real competition. *Shares* is a weekly magazine with a bright and breezy style, and several well-informed writers and tipsters. It carries a great deal of positive information, and might perhaps prove a share puzzling to some, because it seems to recommend so many shares. But it is worth reading because it provides information about so many companies. *Investor's Week* is another newcomer. A little more serious than *Shares*, it is not so tip-oriented, but still carries a great deal of valuable information and opinions. Get it if you can.

The monthlies are a mixed bag. They come and go. Apart from *The Analyst*, a commendable but costly effort, the glossier and more expensive they get, the further they move from anything of real interest to the share trader. Their production schedules do not help. They often have to prepare features well ahead of publication date. *Money Observer* may be worth picking up.

Highly recommended is *Growth Company Investor*, which now appears every two months. It is the successor to *Small Company Investor*, and is evolving fast, and quite difficult to track. It does not appear on the book stands, but is available by subscription from 020-7323 3636. It also has a web service on www.growthcompany.co.uk. And is has a magazine dealing with the more specialist, higher-risk Ofex stocks. That is called OffExchange. Details on the phone number above.

The Tip Sheets

Tip sheets are particularly prominent in the penny share field. When markets are strong, they advertise extensively with lists of winners showing spectacular gains. They are good value. The gains they show in their tables are real. If they say they tipped a share at a particular price, and it has soared since, then tip it they did. Follow the right ones among their tips, and you can make a lot of money. The two main sheets, the *Penny Share Guide* (tel: 0171-447 4040) and *Penny Share Focus* both contain intelligent, valuable research, and put a wealth of information about penny shares before their subscribers. In the late Nineties, they changed editors, generally for the better. Tom Winnifrith's *Red Hot Penny Shares* is an interesting new entrant from an experienced financial journalist with a strong analytical background.

One snag is that the tip sheets provide almost too much. Their enthusiastic tone is encouraging – who would want it any other way? It is tempting to throw money at almost any of their recommendations, to rush into all of them. Because they cover so many shares, they must hit a high proportion of the big winners. But that is not the same as saying that a high proportion of their tips are big winners. It is not that easy.

The other problem, increasingly awkward when markets are booming, is that market-makers read the tip sheets. As with newspaper tips, they often mark prices up before anyone can possibly deal. And the tips tend to spur such a rush of buying that prices roar away from the instant the market opens. The lucky few who manage to buy at close to the recommended price can often sell at once, with a handsome profit.

That said, penny share sheets are worth having. Watch especially for cut-price introductory offers. They are a great source of ideas, and come preciously near to essential for those who wish to play in a bull market, simply because there are days when they send a few shares soaring and leave newspaper commentators baffled about what is going on. If you are sitting on your favourite penny share, and see it take off suddenly on a tip, you need to know what is being said. Otherwise you could be tempted out too quickly. Or you may think you know better than the tip sheet, and can seize an opportunity to take a profit.

There are other tip sheets selling by subscription, and they also feature penny shares from time to time. The *Fleet Street Letter* (tel: 0171-447 4040) is usually sound. *Techinvest* has won a good reputation, concentrating on high-tech stocks where expert advice is particularly important. Investment guru Jim Slater started a tip sheet in the late Nineties. Slater is always worth heeding.

Hargreaves Lansdown (01179 767 767), the independent financial advice firm, offers a number of useful publications at modest prices. And although it is not specifically aimed at penny shares, their AIM Insight newsletter is also recommended. It reproduces articles from the AIM Bulletin, which is written by one of the bright young men at internet experts Durlacher.

I also like *The Small Cap Review* and the *AIM Newsletter*. Though they are not confined to penny shares, and they are only on subscription, they are worth watching if you can get them. Details from 01303 230046.

If you do follow tip sheet ideas, be sure to give your broker clear instructions on how to deal for you. Do give your broker a limit – within, say, 10% or 15% of the price recommended by the tip sheet. Leave the wilder prices to others. Sometimes – but not always – prices settle back a while after the tip appears, and come within a more reasonable buying range. If not, too bad. You cannot win them all. In buoyant markets, the tips can be self-fulfilling, attracting so much buying that the shares perform on the strength of the tip alone, with no real substance to carry the price on. So be careful.

Tip sheets sometimes have a dubious reputation, with suggestions that the writers buy the shares before sending out recommendations, then sell on the rise. It happens, perhaps, but less frequently than popular opinion suggests. Most tip sheets have strict dealing codes. I believe most conduct their affairs honestly and fairly. I would advise anyone very strongly, however, against taking the slightest notice of newsletters with an address outside the United Kingdom, whether they are sent out free, or on subscription. Invariably they are used to trap mug punters, and ease the way for a phone call from some shady share dealer who will try to sell stock in an overseas dud. Have nothing to do with them.

Try to check who publishes any newsletter you may receive. Several are linked to investment advisers or financial companies of one sort or another. That may not necessarily be a bad thing. But do make sure you know who you are dealing with, and what sort of axe they may have to grind.

Other Sources of Information

Inspiration for investment ideas is all around you. In the Eighties, I spotted the sensational transformation of J. Hepworth into high-flying High Street fashion group Next near the beginning of a big share price surge, by reading a woman's magazine and asking questions around the City. Clues to my success with Applied Holographics came from the pages of a popular science magazine. In the spring of 1995, I tipped Unipalm in the *Daily Mail*. Then it was the only UK public company which acted as a service provider giving companies access to the internet. This links computers around the world, and was the subject of endless comment early in 1995. Within six weeks of my recommendation, the price had doubled, even though it had made very little progress in the previous nine months. Suddenly the internet had become a hot investment topic. Nine months later, Unipalm received a bid at more than four times my recommended price.

It is all grist to the mill, and trade magazines can be a valuable source of advance information if you are following a company in a particular industry. *Construction Journal*, for example, is an excellent source of early gossip about building and construction companies. Computer magazines can give useful information on many of the hottest stocks in the market. Sadly, though, there are none I can recommend. There are so many that I cannot sort the good from the bad, and am still trying to get to grips with what it all really means. You should try it, too.

Your local library may house some of these magazines. If you live in London, the business library in the City is invaluable. Major libraries carry *Exchange Telegraph*, or Extel cards. These give a potted history of every quoted company in a form which you will quickly learn to unravel. They show past profits, the registered address of the company (where you should write for a copy of the last published report and accounts), a potted balance sheet, and a list of major shareholders. McCarthy cards are similar.

There are other information services in some libraries, plus the *Stock Exchange Weekly Official List*, showing all share prices, plus dealings by directors. The *Stock Exchange Official Yearbook* is a bumper effort, with outline histories of quoted companies. There is an increasing number of other reference books.

On the whole, these are not worth buying. They date quickly. Pester your bank or broker – whoever deals for you – to get you copies of Extel or McCarthy cards, and anything in his library. Once again, if you can afford it, *Company REFS* is best.

Ask your broker if you can have a copy of the monthly *Stock Exchange Investment List*. This is a pocket-size, cheaply-produced booklet with details of all listed securities, giving the amount of issued capital, when dividends are due, the last dividend payment, a rough price range, the dividend yield, and the price high and low in the last year or two. The prices are only a rough guide. A few brokers send them out without charge. As a basic reference, they are invaluable.

If you want to try to keep in touch through each day, the Ceefax and Teletext services come free on TV sets with Teletext. They provide a reasonable service, though the range of prices and other information is patchy, and penny shares are unlikely to feature much. Better than nothing, though.

The Internet

The growth of the internet has sparked a revolution for small investors, allowing them immediate access to much of the information which drives the City professionals. In a way, it should come at the top of any section dealing with sources of information, though I know that many people are not yet connected.

If you intend to be even half-serious about the investment game, you must get on the net. Instead of gambling on your next penny share, take the cash and buy a computer, and a modem, and link up to the net. Installing it can be a touch tricky, so talk to the salesman and pick a package which makes connecting simple. With colour coded plugs and switches, it is getting easier.

Access to a whole new world of information might change much more than just your investment outlook. If you have children, do it anyway. Being internet literate will be vital for their future.

The net has transformed investment opportunities. As we entered the New Millennium, I wrote a new book *The £1,000 Share Punter* (Laddingford Books, P0 Box 488, Yalding, ME18 6BJ, price £12.99, not available in book shops) especially to deal with the new band of small investors using the net to gamble on shares. With that book or without it, you can join in and exploit the openings on hand in this exciting new era.

There are internet sites offering financial information springing up all of the time. Most tend to have the tag ".co.uk" or ".com" at the end. Do not overlook those dots. The .co.uk sites tend to be UK based, and may sometimes be local variations of US sites, which tend to have ".com" on the end. If one suffix does not work, try the other. Several carry a wealth of financial news, up-dated through the day, and can be accessed at no extra cost. Perhaps the busiest is linked to Freeserve, though you do not have to be connected to Freeserve to get to it. It is available on www.ukinvest.com. It carries news, delayed share prices, and a variety of columnists (at the time of writing, I am one of them).

There are several other similar sites worth visiting. Try www.Citywire.com, or www.thestreet.co.uk. To get most of these services, you have to do nothing more than type in the address. Some ask you to give your name, address and e-mail address. Others will ask you to subscribe for parts of the service – often if you want to upgrade to real-time prices.

One I recommend is www.nothing-ventured.co.uk from stockbrokers Durlacher. For an extra subscription, it allows you the chance of getting in on their public flotations, though these are unlikely to be in penny shares. There is a great deal of free information on www.hemscott.com, or www.digitallook.com, or www.moneyworld.co.uk.

Company announcements are sometimes free, sometimes require a fee for instant access. Look at www.iii.co.uk, or www.sharepages.com.

Many brokers offer access to sites with all sorts of information, if you deal with them. For all-round instant information, you may well have to pay around £10 a month subscription. I have not sampled the www.hemscott.com site. but it looks as if it is pretty comprehensive. I use www.etrade.co.uk.

A number of newspaper have their own sites, though I find I do not use them much. But you can get www.ft.com, or www.telegraph.co.uk. The *Daily Mail* is dabbling in all sorts of confusing odds and ends. There is one called www.thisismoney.co.uk. Somewhere in it you will find my share tipping columns.

Several sites allow you to create your own list of investments, and will update the prices and values as the day goes by. That is very useful, and helps if you are attempting to follow a stop-loss system (more later). You can do this on www.moneyworld.co.uk, or www.nothing-ventured.co.uk, or on www.iii.co.uk. It is developing so fast, that by the time you read this, there may be many others.

Some sites will e-mail you alerts when there is information relating to your stocks. Others will e-mail you there daily bulletins. These include www.ukinvest.com, www.iii.co.uk, www.moneyworld.co.uk, and www.moneynet.com from Reuters.

One of the most fascinating developments in the internet revolution is the rise of message boards, or bulletin boards. These allow investors to swap ideas. You can ask questions, post opinions, or try to ramp shares simply by joining one of the sites, getting a user name (not your own normally), and writing what you think. It will appear on the message board for all to see.

Some of it is nonsense, some naïve, some intended to mislead, and some very well-informed indeed. You need to be careful, and there has been the usual call for regulation from busy-bodies who want the nanny state to supervise all we do. But bulletin boards are a marvellous source of fun and information. I have picked up stories for use in the *Daily Mail*, and the idea for a couple of extremely successful share tips.

The most fun, and wildest, is on www.hemscott.com. Look for the information exchange. There is a good bulletin board on www.moneyworld.co.uk. The www.iii.co.uk is more difficult to access, and if you are not careful, you will get into a system which bombards you with hundreds of e-mails. The Etrade board is very well-informed, and there is a good one at www.citybull.co.uk. I also applaud a newcomer www.investorevolution.co.uk and hope it gets established.

Finally, I am also up there on the internet. I have my own comment site at www.michaelwalters.com. By the time you read this, there might also be a message board. Whatever you do, do not miss out on the internet. It has become a vital tool for investors.

SEVEN

The Penny Share Shells

*

Slim penny shares can be transformed into heavyweight superstars for a variety of reasons. Much the most common, though, is because a vigorous new management team steps in and takes the old company by the scruff of the neck, shakes it up, kicks out the rubbish, and starts again.

Nothing works as well as often as the old shell game. Take one of the living dead out of the company casualty ward, and inject it with a bunch of fast-growing businesses, pushing the share price on and up with each successive deal.

The ideal candidate for such treatment, as we have seen, has a low share price, modest market value, solid assets, and a modest share capital where control can be procured without too much expense or difficulty. Corporate finance departments, merger brokers, stockbrokers and enterprising managers comb share lists all of the time, hunting suitable companies. Look for clues along the lines set out in earlier chapters, and you will have a fair idea of what they are looking for. If you are confident enough to back your own judgement, you should move in and sit with the shares. That will give you the biggest profit, if you are right. But it is often possible to clamber aboard just as the action starts, before the market has spotted the full potential behind the first deal and realised just how much it could mean.

Backing the New Boys – Second Chance Time

Second chance time comes by backing the new boys as they arrive, either to take their first share stake or increase it. They usually do it by selling a company into the shell, or by issuing new shares to raise extra money. It will be done with as little fuss as possible. They do not want the shares racing away when they and their partners are stuffing their pockets with stock at the lowest price they can get away with. A roar-away price might suit them later, but when they are selling something to the company, they want the shares as low as possible. That means they get more shares, and can take a bigger slug for themselves.

This 'boarding' operation will be as stealthy as possible. The full story will not appear in the published documents. Stock Exchange rules conveniently do not encourage it. Rosy projections are not allowed for fear of misleading shareholders, raising hopes too high. And, since details of all deals which are under way or in contemplation at the time of the first deal must be disclosed in that first document, the players have to be able to swear hand on heart that there are, indeed, no other deals on the way, so perhaps you should not get too excited. The truth is, of course, that a good team will have a string of possible deals stretching over the horizon. But because of the Stock Exchange ruling, and because they do not want to give too much away, they have been quietly set aside – for the moment. Once the boys have their shares, and the boarding operation is approved by shareholders, it is back to business again, full steam ahead.

No-one is fooled much by this, of course. But it is surprising how often the new boarders can move in fairly quietly if circumstances are right. In the roaring bull markets of 1987, it was much more difficult for them to escape notice because investors had become so attuned to penny share possibilities. Quite a few sneaked in when markets were gloomy in the early Nineties. These days, small investors are growing more sophisticated, more alert. Few new arrivals escape attention. But it can happen if they move when the market is having one of its periodic panics and no-one wants to know about anything positive. So stay vigilant.

The arrival of a new team may well spark a price rise of 20% or more. From time to time, though, some arrive as companies disclose grim profits, and it is difficult to disentangle the ambitious new operators from board changes induced simply by the struggle to survive. Others are unknown, untried names, with no past record to catch the eye. Backing them is more of a gamble, but the entry price might be more modest.

There is always a new stream of players ready to exploit the shell game. Watch for share stakes and new names, and you may have several weeks to climb aboard a penny share shell just as it gets under way. In extreme cases, it may mean paying up to double the price before the action started, but never mind. At this stage, what really matters is the market capitalisation of the vehicle – the size of the company – and the quality of the new team and their supporters.

Usually, even the capitalisation will not matter, so long as it has not got too large. Though the shares may have doubled, if you still have a vehicle valued at under £10 million, you have little to fear. Do not misunderstand. You could still lose all of your investment.

You are taking a gamble – buying any share just after it has doubled obviously seems to carry a greater risk than if it had not doubled. That may be so. But not necessarily. Look upon the extra cost as a sort of insurance premium or as a way of recognising the potential value of new management. If you had been sitting in a penny stock where nothing was happening, just drifting along, the risk of hitting the rocks may have been greater than paying double and knowing at least that a new captain had taken the wheel, backed by a bright new crew. They might run the ship aground more quickly. But the odds are that they will sail it towards a brighter future. That will certainly be their plan. Why else would they be risking their cash?

Nautical nonsense aside, what matters is that if the market value of the company is still £10 million or less, there is lots of room to go higher. It is still small enough for relatively modest deals to make a big impact on the overall value. Another good £10 million deal – not too difficult to find – would double it. If the market value was already up to £30 million, the impact would be less, and finding the right deal could be more difficult. The smaller the base, the easier it is to make it grow. Again, there are no set rules. Use your common sense.

Judging the Quality

It is tempting to suggest that, at the beginning, all you really need is a deal of some sort, never mind the quality. In an overheated market especially, this will be true. Almost anything will do. No-one goes into a new company without some supporters, people he has been able to persuade to believe in him. They will generate enough excitement to send the shares up for a while, no matter how inept their hero. You will make money following suit, if you are quick enough getting in and early enough getting out. It is no joke. Even in the brightest of markets, some no-hopers, clueless clowns, cheats and villains do get into the shell game. They appear to prosper for a while, then flop. Every one might look like a winner for a little while. But be warned. Some will run the company aground more quickly and surely than ever. And they will be gone before you realise it.

What you really want is quality, a new team which is going to stick around and build a worthwhile business, making a small fortune for you while they make a larger fortune for themselves. You do not want a shell which makes a brief run and then fades. The big money comes not from doubling up in six months, but from doubling and doubling again. Then, perhaps, doubling yet again. Look at the tables of top performing shares each year. It does happen. So if you spot the potential big winner, stay with it. That is the one which will turn your £1,000 into £10,000, your £5,000 into £50,000 – not the quick in and out deals at a few hundred pounds profit in half a dozen small situations.

So watch for details of what is afoot. The fine print can be vitally important, and when your money is riding on it, you will find it easier to summon the energy to read it and think about it. The *Financial Times* usually carries more of the fine print on more deals than anyone. But for the serious penny punter, it is inadequate. The analysis and comment which comes at the end of the week in the *Investors Chronicle* may sometimes be more informative, with a little background on the record of the new team, and some clues as to what the deal may mean. But there is no substitute for getting hold of the document yourself and going through it. Ring the company secretary, or the bank advising on the deal. Or perhaps the public relations firm.Or go to the company's website.

Even that may mean you have missed out, not just on the first stage, but on some of the second stage. The routine varies. Some opportunities go almost totally unreported, because no press release is issued, quite deliberately. For example, in the *Daily Mail* one year, I nominated a little company called LDH Holdings as my share of the year. The price was 44p. It appeared the ideal penny vehicle. It had a sound, profitable textile trading company, a good slug of cash, and a chairman who controlled the shares but was reputed to be interested in doing deals to help the company grow more quickly. One investor had a 5% stake. I knew him as a bright, careful deal-maker.

The price moved up to around 50p after my tip, then hovered around 55p for months, with help from promising interim profit figures. I was out of the country for most of April. On my return, I noticed that the shares had run to 65p. Something was afoot. I made a call or two, but discovered nothing. My broker said that there had been nothing to account for the share rise.

Early one May morning, there was an announcement. Three investors had bought 22% of the company at 50p a share, with the chairman's blessing. One was a merchant banker with a first-class reputation, one a former managing director of Marks & Spencer, and the other the deal-maker who already had a small stake.

The shares flew to 130p. No press release was sent out. The company saw no need for publicity. Because I had tipped LDH, I wrote a short piece, telling readers to hold on. Two other newspapers carried the sparsest details, with no attempt at explaining what was afoot. The shares went to 155p.

Later, they topped 340p without much happening. Then the mood changed, the market crashed, and they tumbled. The company was taken over for around 130p, a sensible price given the trading strength it had gathered by then.

The story is not meant to crow because I sort of picked a winner. It illustrates a number of the lessons which are there to be learnt in the penny share game. The company was right originally because it was small, had strong assets in cash, a sound trading base, and a good chunk of its shares in the hands of someone who might do a deal.

Those clues apart, the message came loud and clear to any who were awake to receive it when the deal-maker popped up, in public, with a 5% stake. Why would he be committing cash to a no-hoper?

After that, it was just a matter of time. It took a few months. The share price gave a clear signal when it ran to 65p for no apparent reason. Anyone watching the screen would have noticed more business than usual on some days. Whenever the price eased a penny or two, it perked up again later. I still do not know who was picking up the shares. It was not the boarding party. But somehow, someone had got wind of something, and was quietly tucking shares away. There was another clue, too, of course, for the small share punter. For better or for worse, the shares had featured in the *Mail*, long before the action happened. It pays to heed the press, sometimes.

The LDH story is interesting too, because it shows the problems of keeping up with events. If you had access to a price screen, it would have been possible to buy immediately after the announcement at 120p or 130p. Relying on more conventional sources of information, you could well have missed the deal altogether. It showed up later in the *Stock Exchange Weekly Official Intelligence*, but that week's *Investors Chronicle* missed it. When I spoke to two of the new stakeholders, they talked quite freely, but said they had no deals planned and were not anxious to attract attention.

Their reticence was, perhaps, an extreme example of how quiet things can sometimes be kept. Because they were simply buying a stake, not going beyond the 29.9% point, after which they would have been required to make a bid to all shareholders or get Takeover Panel exemption, they had no need to send a document to shareholders. Nor even pen a press release.

Perhaps the most important lesson of all, though, is one I deal with in my chapter on selling. Anyone who held when the shares were going up, resisting early temptations to take profits, would have done very well – but only if they had sold at higher levels. The shares topped 340p. Anyone running a stop-loss system (more of that later) would have sold on a 10% fall (at about 310p), or certainly on a 20% fall (at around 280p) and would have done very well. Those who sat and watched as the shares retraced their rise would have ended up cursing themselves.

Tackling the Deal Documents

Most moves into a shell will require at least a document to shareholders. It may be preceded by a press release, though sometimes the two go out together. Sometimes, there is no press release. Sometimes, the press is given the barest bones, and sometimes there is a full explanation. Often the detailed document is not sent to the press at all. Even when it is, pressure on time and space may mean it is overlooked. Who worries about a small deal in a small company, involving names no-one much knows?

That is a frustration for penny share watchers. But, once again, ignorance creates the opportunity. The fewer people who see the chance, the greater the scope for the alert investor to take a position before the price moves and the rest of the world wakes up.

So watch the small print in the newspapers. Ask your broker to tell you every time something happens in any company which interests you. He may not do it. But ask. If you have a lively broker, he will be as keen as you to spot the chance of getting in on the action at the beginning. You will be helping each other. He needs ideas for himself and his other clients. But make sure he talks to you first.

Once you spot the action, contact the company secretary. Ask them to send you any relevant documents. They should do it. If you cannot get them, contact the merchant bankers to the company if there are any, or the brokers. In the last resort, Extel will be preparing a card carrying the latest details. Ask your broker or dealer to get one – though it takes longer. Or perhaps a copy of the analysis report which brokers who use the system can have printed out in the office almost instantly. Or search the internet.

Following the Money

There are all sorts of clues in official documents. The unshakeable rule, though, is to follow the money. See who is putting in how much, at what price, and what they get in return. More than anything, that will indicate how serious the new players are. There is nothing like having your own money at risk. From your point of view, the more the players have at stake, the better.

Check to see if they have bought shares already. There is always a section in company reports listing deals by the directors and their associates in the previous twelve months, and any dealings by the new team. Check the prices they have paid, and just what has happened. There is also a list of the interests of the main shareholders – plus details of what shares will go to the new people as a result of the deal in progress. If there are options giving them further shares at a future date, read carefully. They may be linked to profit targets for the main company, or the company they are bringing in. Those targets will give you a valuable clue as to what is expected. If all goes to plan, you can expect any forecasts to be well beaten, so as to allow the new boys to take up the maximum number of extra shares. You can be sure they will be doing everything they can to meet those targets. It is all common sense. You want to see as much commitment as possible. The more carrots the better, and the longer they ensure the directors stay interested, the better. Long contracts of employment – three years maximum, though there is a fuss about anything over two years in big companies – are a help, too, in small shell-style companies.

Do not, though, assume it is all there, made easy for you. Read, and think about it. Follow the route of the deals from page to page, and cross check. Take the trouble to consult the foot-notes, and pursue the cross-references. Sometimes it seems that they are made complicated on purpose, to obscure and confuse. Remember that these documents are put together by the players and their advisers. Official red tape may force much complication – but there is always a fair amount of leeway in deciding how things are presented. So-called facts and figures can be manipulated – and they often are. The longer you look at the City, the more you appreciate that the day-to-day reality is very different from its formal face and the way the world is supposed to work.

Look at the details of the material contracts carefully. Compare them with what goes earlier. They list relevant deals in the previous twelve months. See whether the assets which are being traded now were originally bought at the same price, if there was an earlier deal involving those assets. See who is taking a profit on them. Sometimes the answers can be disturbing. Every now and then, something which requires more explanation pops up. Sometimes you will find that the boys going in are selling assets which they bought earlier and more cheaply themselves, and there is no good reason for the higher price they are charging now.

Is that good? Probably not. It might give you a clue as to the integrity of the players, how ready they are to bend things to suit their book. That makes your judgement very tricky. If you think they have pulled off an unduly favourable deal for themselves, should you walk away? Or should you reflect that these people are determined to make money, and may well make it for shareholders in the process?

This causes me great difficulty. Obviously, I disapprove of manipulation. In the long run, it almost invariably comes unstuck. In the short term, though, the players may succeed in generating enough hype to send the share price usefully ahead. It may pay to stick with the less scrupulous managers for a while, simply because they will manipulate the price higher. Make your own judgement. For my part, I prefer to steer clear of such operators and such dubious chances of gain. Such people do not deserve to succeed – and when they go wrong, anyone holding the shares might find they slump without warning.

When you are reading the fine print, you should also check for restrictions on future share sales. Often there will be an undertaking not to sell for twelve months or more, or until certain profit targets have been achieved. Does that mean the new team intends to get out quickly? Or is it just that they might need to pay off the borrowings they have undertaken to buy in to start with? It may be impossible to discover. Think about it. Could it mean that a year hence, there will be a lot of shares looking for a buyer? Sensibly, the regulations for the AIM companies normally ban directors from selling any shares within two years if the company is raising money.

The Deal Price

Pay attention to the price being paid for any company which is going in. Often the new team will be taking their share stake in exchange for a business which they own. The conflict of interest is quite instructive. There is a temptation to value the new company highly, to ensure that the new players get as many shares as they can. If they charge too much, however, it will be seen as a bad deal for the old shareholders. Payment by results is often the best compromise, with some shares to the new team at the start, and more later if their company meets profit targets. Obviously, though, valuing a new business at a higher than average price earnings ratio for quoted companies in the same line of operation is not a good idea.

The Rights Price

If the new team are launching a rights issue, raising fresh capital for the company, and allowing themselves and their supporters to take up new shares in one swoop, check the price again. It will almost certainly be higher than the share price a few months earlier, before anyone got wind of their intentions. It may well be lower than the price immediately before the deal was announced, simply because the news may have leaked and pushed the price up, or the team and their friends have been buying. It may not make much difference in the long term, but you will feel happier knowing the price was not pumped up too much in advance to make the first deal look right.

All being well, you should take up as many shares as you can in the new issue. It is sensible to consider the probable price after the deal, the ex-rights price, as you do so. Take, for example, a company where the price was 65p ahead of the action. A new team is taking stock at 40p, but such is the power of their reputation that the price in the market has gone to 150p. That may look an extreme example when markets are uncertain, but in good times that kind of rise can happen. There is a two-for-one rights issue at 40p, qualifying for our penny share class even though the market price is out of reach.

Do the sums. Buy one share at 150p, and you have the right to buy two more at 40p each. Do it, and you will have three shares which have cost you 230p (150p, plus 40p, plus 40p). That means you are effectively paying just under 77p a share when you buy the shares cum (with rights) at 150p. Not quite so comfortable for penny punters, but worth considering – and very different from 150p.

Open Offers

Virtually all of the remarks which apply to rights issues apply to open offers and claw-back opportunities. An open offer is similar to a rights issue. It allows you the opportunity to buy new shares in the company in a proportion related to the number of shares you already hold. It lets the company raise new money, and allows new managers to buy in and increase their stake. The difference between a rights issue and an open offer is simply that the new shares do not just go to existing investors. The company normally gets the whole issue underwritten – it lines up investors who will buy the shares whatever happens – and gives existing shareholders the chance to 'claw back', or take for themselves, some of the shares otherwise due to go to the underwriters.

There may be accounting advantages for the company, but the main reason for an open offer rather than a rights issue is that the cash can be raised more quickly, and the underwriting team has more positive support for the company. In some ways, it is a change for the worse, in that it undermines the rights of existing investors to have first call on new shares. If it takes place in your penny share punt, though, forget about that. Claw back as many shares as you can afford if it means a new management team is going in.

Checking the Team – and their Advisers

Obviously the ability of the new men you may be backing is crucial. If they are selling a company in, there will be a section in the back of the document bearing the profit and loss account and balance sheet of that company. Unless it is new, you can get some idea of what sort of business the boys have built, whether it is growing, how strong it is on assets, and such. There should also be a section in the front of the document giving a thumb-nail sketch of their recent careers. Look for the big name experience. Increasingly, middle managers are shifting out of big companies, looking for smaller operations to run themselves, and to make a little cash for themselves. Try to trace it back, and see how important a role they played in any bigger company, how long they were there, why they left. Some of the most interesting company builders in recent years have served their apprenticeship at Hanson – Greg Hutchings of Tomkins, of course. Or the boys behind Wassall.

Sad to say, potted histories sometimes leave out important chunks. AIM companies have strict disclosure rules on the history of directors. Sadly, others do not, though the AIM idea may push bigger companies to follow. Outside AIM, there are still times when involvement in troubled companies is somehow overlooked. And when a brief spell with a big name is included, without any indication of how long it lasted. A glance at the *Directory of Directors*, which you will find in most decent libraries, will help. Ask your broker. Search the internet. Ask anyone you think might know. Look in the relevant trade press. Watch the newspapers for snatches of gossip. It is not easy to be sure. You will have to take much on trust. Watch the age, too. A young man might lack experience, and an old man might be too lacking in enterprise. Tread carefully with anyone under, say, 28. Or over 52. Those figures are arbitrary. They have no special magic. But they are about right.

The Backing Group

The quality of their supporters is important, too. The bigger the merchant bank or broker advising on the deal, the better. Or the nominated adviser if you are looking at an AIM company. Blue bloods do not take on new, smaller clients lightly. If they do, there is a special reason. Not only should the managers be exceptional, but the placing power, the money available to the managers to get the business moving ahead, will be exceptional. But there are some lively, small houses who can get shares motoring. They specialise in ferreting out suitable shell companies, and offering them to bright new managers. They make a profit providing the shares for the team to start with, and take fees for advice along the way.

One or two tend to specialise in the quick turn, and there are question marks about their ability to sustain the action. They get a shell up and running, take big profits for themselves at the start, then drift away as the company loses momentum. Look at what the advisers have done before, and see how share prices have performed there. You will soon spot the questionable dealers.

Do not overlook advisers from outside London. The skills of Scotland's money managers seem to have been lacking in this area so far, but there are enterprising broking firms in Manchester, Bristol and Birmingham with a talent for spotting opportunities in local companies.

What Next?

Look carefully, and you will find clues about what is to happen next. Remember, the new team do not want to attract too much attention. But they do not want to appear dead-beats. And the outgoing directors will want to give some signals to shareholders, and will be anxious to be seen to have done a good deal. So some goodies may go into the shop window.

Part of the normal routine is for new managers to be required to make a bid to all shareholders at the price they have paid for their shares, if they are taking more than 29.9% of the company. Normally, this bid will be a formality, well below the market price. The board will recommend the deal, but will advise shareholders to sell in the market or consult their advisers. That is a clear sign that you should stay on for the ride.

Less obviously, however, any deal document will carry little pointers. Take an actual example from a few years back. The shares were comfortably in the penny class for weeks after plans for the first deal were aired, and still there two weeks after the document went to shareholders. But if you looked carefully, the message was clear.

The team selling a new company in agreed not to sell any shares for three years without board approval. They would take more if the company met future profit targets. The proposed acquisition "marks a major step forward" for the public company, which "will be well placed to grow both organically and by acquisition". The new directors had built a company with significant assets and profits over the previous two years, making 17 trading acquisitions. They would be involved in an executive capacity for ten working days a month "initially". They would assist in supervising the company's recovery from its present situation "and the identification and negotiation of potential acquisitions". And so on.

Although there was no press release to suggest anything exciting, and the acquisition looked relatively routine, anyone who took the trouble to read through the details could hardly miss the message. Here were two new men, backed by the existing big shareholders, who would launch this company on a programme of acquisitions. Their experience was not great (both were in their early thirties), but they had put together a private company by a rapid series of deals. Now they would try again, in a public company. There was no guarantee that they would get it right – but the odds were interesting and exciting. Just the kind of thing which might make a penny share winner. It was all there, spelt out fairly clearly for anyone who read the document carefully and digested just what it said.

That little gem was in front of me when I wrote an earlier edition of this book. It showed all of the signs of a potential penny share winner, worth repeating as an example of what to watch out for. Updating this book later, I should report that the boys got the shell going nicely, with a 50% rise in the share price. Then it began to emerge that some of their acquisitions were not so smart. It turned bad. They ended up selling out, barely ahead of their entry price.

Despite the disappointment, the story is valuable because it illustrates the opportunities and the dangers in penny shares. No matter how convincing the initial attractions may appear, the best-laid plans can go wrong. And they do. If you wanted to get out ahead, it was also important to run a stop-loss system – the profit-taking scheme detailed later in this book.

Patience And Persistence

Getting it right requires a combination of patience and persistence. Deals do not always happen when you expect them. Delays crop up time and again. You may be aboard a new company with all systems go, and the next big deal could fall through at the last minute, so they need to start again. If nothing happens in six months, worry. Start to ask questions. Think about selling if you do not get answers which make sense.

And all of the way, from the first moment you get a clue that something may be about to happen, be persistent. Company directors will not thank me for it, but I am often surprised by small shareholders who contact me with questions, and who reveal that they found out something or other by talking or writing to the chairman. It takes a little nerve, and will not always work. But if you cannot find out what you need to know, ring the chairman, or the managing director. Or write and ask. You never know what will happen. If nothing else, just seeing how you are treated – even if you draw a blank – could give you some interesting ideas about the company and the people behind it.

Third Time Lucky

Opportunities for making money in the shell game wax and wane. In the year 2000, they look good, though the supply of such companies has been shrinking fast. Dozens have been mopped up and transformed into internet flyers – or flyers for a while, at least. Some of the less obvious candidates are emerging as players because directors are beginning finally to accept that they must do something. It is important to get in early if you can, but there may be more than one chance of leaping aboard a shell. On the second, or even the third deal, there could still be time enough to get lucky.

The chances are created because the Stock Exchange rarely approves a radical change of direction in a quoted company without it going through procedures which amount almost to a new flotation. So shells tend to be shifted gradually from one area of operation to another, built deal by deal to a size where they can do the big one. This may involve several small to medium acquisitions, each with a document outlining how things are going. And perhaps two or three fund-raising moves.

Sometimes the extra cash will come in through a general rights issue. Increasingly, companies have moved towards open offers, the special subscription deals, with supporters lined up to take shares. In uncertain markets, small companies might not always get their cash from a rights issue. So these open offers have to be marketed quietly in advance to the big money boys.

Insider information? Make up your own mind. Privileged parties are told the game plan, get to interview the new directors, and know where things are supposed to go. In exchange, they may accept some restrictions on their ability to sell. They also sometimes lend a more sophisticated eye to the plans, so small shareholders can feel comfortable that the right investors have backed the issue.

In a way, more subdued conditions suit sober penny share players better. They help produce a higher proportion of committed backers, people aware of taking some greater risk, but open to the opportunity. And when times are harder, the chances of building a quoted vehicle by picking up interesting private companies at a modest price – often from the receiver – are good. The initial penny share price advance may be more subdued, but longer-term prospects are sounder.

Bad is Beautiful

Drawing on the first draft of this book, slightly tongue in cheek, I advanced the theory in the *Mail* in the summer of 1987 – "Bad Is Beautiful". It attracted a lot of comment, and when I first wrote it, it appeared to be working reasonably well.

The notion was that many of the soar-away stocks which figured as big winners in the mid-Eighties had once been companies no respectable fund manager would want to know. Before they got better, they had to get much worse, and the original management would have to be replaced by a new team. In a bull market, hardly any public company could go bust, because as soon as the shares slumped, a new entrepreneur would be bashing at the door, begging to take it over as a vehicle for his public company ambitions.

It almost became a good sign for investors, spotting a company which had been run into the ground, with the board giving up, and selling to a new team. That was how the real high-flyers were born. The worse the company, the better the chances of revitalisation, and substantial growth in the shares.

I advanced the theory with a little grin, ready to challenge conventional investment standards. In the late Eighties and early Nineties, the theory wore thin. One small company after another went to the wall, and promoters lost interest in problem companies as a cheap way into the game.

In recent years, however, I have begun to wonder about it again. Many small companies have displayed a remarkable resilience and determination. Some are just clinging on. Sometimes they look ideal for the shell game – with the controlling shareholders understanding only too well that their best chance of making real money is to support new management in reshaping the company.

So, without advancing it too seriously, "Bad Is Beautiful" may have some validity. Think about it. Do not place too much faith in it, but keep it in the back of your mind. Few thriving quoted companies will be willing to let control pass to a new player. The best targets may be among those which have had their difficulties, have kept a few decent assets intact, and have survived long enough to let someone else carry on the fight.

The shell game never dies – sometimes bad can be beautiful, after all.

EIGHT

Other Penny Opportunities

✸

Most penny winners come from spotting a share which is ripe for the attentions of a promising new management team – but not all of them. There are fortunes to be made by catching a recovery stock just before the recovery begins, by picking a share in a cyclical industry as it hits bottom, by gambling on a new venture in the early stages, by backing a new product or direction, or by riding a new issue as it grows. The brave – or foolish – can make a fortune dabbling in Australian, Canadian, or Irish mining stocks, or something with nifty under-exploited assets out in South America or what once was way behind the Iron Curtain – though I would never recommend it.

Many of the clues and qualities discussed in earlier chapters can be applied to spotting any sort of successful penny share. Obviously, you need to start with a low price, and preferably a modest stock market capitalisation. The more assets, the merrier. The more easily you can trade in the shares, the safer you are.

Recovery Shares

There is an especially close link between the recovery share and the asset injection company, the shell company. Clearly, it does not matter much what you call them, so long as you make money. I make my distinctions in this book in the hope of making things clearer. If you find the names confusing, take no notice. What effectively distinguishes an asset injection company from a recovery stock is really a confession of defeat by the old management. They recognise they cannot turn the company around, cannot make too much more at it, so they sell out to someone else and allow them to try, often starting with a completely new business alongside the remnants of the old.

An experienced management does fight back, sometimes with startling results. For the penny share punter, however, it does not matter much whether the managers win or lose, so long as the underlying company has something going for it. The failed recovery stock often becomes the shell opportunity for another set of managers, so the risk of the whole thing collapsing completely and investors needing to write off the share value altogether is fairly small. Back a share for its recovery potential and it hardly matters if it goes wrong at first – someone will step in and transform it, so long as it does not have a crippling burden of debt.

In the mid-Eighties, it was almost more rewarding for shareholders to see the old management throw in the towel. The share gain generated by new players with a fresh reputation comes through more quickly and dramatically than anything inspired by a plucky fight-back to health under an established board. The old team always has a struggle to regain credibility. Perhaps that brings us back to "Bad is beautiful" again.

What you want when picking a penny recovery stock is exactly what forms the main virtue of any good penny stock – assets, assets, and more assets. The greater the assets, the longer the company can fight on, and the greater its appeal to a new team should anything go really wrong.

Perhaps the most remarkable recovery stock of all in recent years has been First National Finance Corporation, the credit company run by Pat Matthews in the early Seventies. With the secondary banking collapse of 1974, First National plunged desperately into debt. It owed hundreds of millions to the Bank of England Lifeboat, a lending operation set up to prevent a whole fleet of smaller banking businesses sinking. First National Ordinary shares were worthless by any normal measure at one stage. It was easy to buy them by the bucket-load for 1p or less in 1975. The Bank of England drafted in tough new managers, and most thought the plan was to knock the business back into sufficient shape to sell it to a bigger brother. But the rescuers rowed on and on. By the summer of 1987, First National Finance was still with us, and the shares were trading at more than 300p – a recovery stock indeed.

First National survived because it had powerful friends – the most powerful. The Bank of England could not let it fail, and extended it loans to ensure that it survived. Powerful friends are important. Check the list of shareholders in any ailing company you fancy. If the likes of the Prudential Assurance, Hermes (the British Telecom and Post Office pension funds), Legal

& General, or unit trust group M&G are there, take heart. They do not like backing losers. They will work behind the scenes to ensure that appropriate managers are recruited, new systems are devised, and that the business bites the bullet and closes chronic loss-makers. Above all, they will make sure there is sufficient finance at the right time. They may extract a heavy price, but will do their damndest to see it sorted out in the interests of everyone.

That gives a useful clue when it comes to hunting suitable shares. Get a copy of the annual report to unit-holders in the M&G Recovery Trust. The managers of this fund have displayed a rare knack for backing companies when they are down, and either watching them recover, or supporting them through their recovery schemes. Their list of investments, sent to unit-holders every six months, is a treasure-trove of recovery stocks – though M&G are patient, long-term investors. Do not count on short-term fireworks, and do not expect them to get every one right.

You may not be able to tell which shares the big pension funds own. They usually hide behind nominee names. But all of the unit trusts, and the investment trusts, list their portfolios in their own reports. Most are ready to back companies which go wrong, if they have shares in them. Look through unit trust portfolios for low-priced shares. They will be there for a reason. Some will be low-priced shares the managers think will grow for normal reasons. Others will be shares which have gone wrong, and have become penny shares since the trust bought them – the losers. Their management may have gone astray, but the big boys may be reluctant to desert them. Increasingly, they are reluctant to let them slide on down into oblivion. So they press for changes, support fresh initiatives, or help to push the recovery ahead in some way.

Before you buy, though, try to ensure that the slide has stopped. Traders talk about the dangers of trying to catch a falling knife. Heed it. You do not want to buy into a falling price and then watch it slump further. Study the report and accounts, anything from the company. Try to identify why things went wrong. You need to establish that clearly in your own mind, so that you can weigh up whether a recovery is actually possible or probable, or whether the company is simply locked into an unstoppable decline. Maybe the market for the group's products has dwindled forever, been stolen by imports, or left behind by fashion or new technology. Maybe the management has lost interest. Maybe the whole business is pretty hopeless, or too heavily burdened with debt to get out from under.

Company profit statements are always out of date and are of limited help. Watch, though, for the trend of profit margins. That can be detected in crude fashion by dividing profits into sales. If the margin has advanced, perhaps the business is beginning to pick up. If sales have fallen, is it because the whole market for such products is in trouble? Or is some special factor involved, peculiar to that company? Anything which looks unusual, and may not happen a second time – perhaps those exceptional items we looked at earlier – can be knocked off the margin calculation. It should not be there next time, so maybe higher profits will come through. Look, too, to see if one area of the business has suffered most of the losses, and is dragging the rest of the company down. Perhaps that could be sold, or closed, transforming the main company's outlook.

If there is a hefty overhanging debt, could it be undone by selling part of the company, and rebuilding the rest? Or if the business was rationalised and reorganised by new managers, could there be large savings in overheads? Or would the problems be solved if a new team could step in with extra cash to refinance the business? Is there any chance that the existing management might work such a miracle?

New recruits may be good news. Family-run businesses do sometimes get tired or too cosy, and sometimes need an injection of fresh blood. Sometimes it takes an outsider to carry through the cuts the old directors know are needed, but lack the heart to make themselves. It is surprising how often a new chief executive can work wonders, tackling old problems with a fresh eye. Suddenly, old ideas are challenged, lingering problems tackled. Watch announcements of board changes, and check the background of any new men. The *Financial Times* is a good place to follow them. Nowadays, it pays much more attention to board changes, and carries a regular useful section which outlines the background of the individuals concerned.

Some directors carry a valuable reputation as company doctors, going from one ailing business to another, often at the behest of big shareholders. They may take their own team in, bring in new systems, clear out the dead wood, and perhaps arrange new financing. Men like David James have gained a formidable reputation for such things. John Jackson is a big institutional favourite. Bob Morton is less a company doctor than a general force for pepping things up in smallish companies, though his record is beginning to look exposed. Paul Johnson's son Luke and partners like Stephen Hargrave and

Hugh Osmond are not renowned for their management skills, but their arrival on a board is usually the signal that there are deals to be done. The appearance of Nigel Wray in any small company is generally good news, while Stuart Wallis is doing well after making a splendid job of turning around Fisons and selling it.

The standard clues are there, though, for other names. Watch whether they take share options, or buy shares for themselves. Look for details of their contracts. Discover if they are leaving senior posts at other big companies, placing a secure future at risk. Measure their commitment.

Cyclical Stocks

Cyclical stocks have many of the same characteristics, but they differ because of the way their fortunes are linked to industries which wax and wane, often with the overall economy. It may seem obvious that house builders, for example, prosper in good economic times, when mortgages are cheap and plentiful and people have more cash to spend. And they suffer when times are hard, interest rates high, and industry is depressed. It does not take a stock market superstar to work that out. But it can be remarkable what a shock the same old routine business cycle can deliver if you are not awake to it. It stands to reason, of course, that house building profits will be under pressure when times are hard. Yet the market always tends to overdo things. Because prices get carried too high when the market is rising, they have further to fall when it goes down. And there is nothing like a falling market to spread gloom and despondency among the sanest of investors. There are times when it seems as if prices will never recover. That, of course, is the time to buy – especially the cyclical stocks.

Fluctuations between the peaks and troughs can be dramatic, even in the shares of first-class companies which will carry on trading forever. Patient investors, who can wait to buy at the bottom and hold on long enough to sell near the top, and then stay out of the market until the bottom is near again, can do very well. But it takes patience and great conviction. The idea of contrary thinking – the time to buy is when everyone else is selling, and vice versa – is popular in the City. Some apply it with great success. Somehow, though, most overlook it most of the time.

It does take real nerve to buy when everyone else is selling. And to sell when the market is soaring. Of course, no-one can be sure when the market has hit bottom, or reached the top. More, though, on that in the section on selling shares.

The cyclical share punter requires a stubborn streak, self-confidence, and a reasonable memory. Go back a while, and it is easy to see that certain industries do go through bad spells, almost as surely as night follows day. Some track the course of the national economy, and others have their own sequence.

As a very good general guide, the health of the economy determines the progress of house builders, building materials suppliers, stores, motor dealers, manufacturers and component makers, packaging materials, papermakers, transport groups and some raw material suppliers. Particular industries also tend to follow a cyclical pattern, sometimes linked to the economy, sometimes less so. Watch computers, electronics, oil, bulk chemicals, insurance, hotels, restaurants, carpets and furniture, and textiles.

Such a list is very primitive, but it provides a starting point, something to think about. In truth, the health of the economy is crucial to almost all companies – though sometimes it may not always be primarily linked to the health of the UK economy. Particular companies in particular industries will always buck the trend, but they will need very special qualities for that to happen.

As ever, you need to ensure that the shares you pick to perk up have as much basic strength as possible. Asset power tops the list, as usual. That is closely followed – and often linked – to sound finance. Businesses buried in debt may not have the capacity to respond to any pick-up in the cycle.

Get it right, and the possibilities are exciting. House builder Barratt Developments went from a low of 38p in 1992 to a peak 220p in 1993. It then dropped back, only to double from peak to trough between 1993 and 1994, before sliding again as the house building industry failed to make the recovery many had been expecting.

Currencies

The boom-bust cycle also applies to sterling. In 1997 and 1998, the air was full of cries of pain from companies which do significant business overseas. They were upset by the strength of sterling against most major currencies. Strong sterling means that anything made in Britain costs more for anyone overseas. It means that British companies either have to cut their prices to stay competitive, or simply lose business. It also means that competitors based in countries with a weak currency gain ground, because their exports look cheaper to foreign buyers. However you slice it, that hammers the profits of UK businesses.

Equally, British companies with extensive operations overseas suffer when the profits they earn appear lower as they are translated into sterling for Stock Exchange requirements. No matter that, in the land where they operate, they might still be doing very well. If most shareholders are in the UK, translating overseas earnings into lower UK profits is what will count.

Inevitably, the strength of sterling is not assured. Unless and until we get into a fixed exchange rate mechanism, some companies will suffer unduly from a strong pound – or benefit from a weak one. So watch the pound. It may offer a purely temporary opportunity for buying into the shares of a business which is fundamentally sound, but merely under a cloud until sterling slides.

New Ventures

New ventures are completely different. They rarely boast any significant asset backing. They have no profit record to speak of, the management may be untried, and the whole thing can resemble the stock market equivalent of a journey into space. A few new ventures will be injected into existing companies, or spun off from established giants to form separate share issues.

New ventures represent a complete gamble. Try to learn what you can about the background to the business in question and to establish the credentials of the people who run it. Make sure they have proper patent protection on their ideas – if they are at a sufficiently advanced stage to qualify for it – check what the competition might be, and try to take a practical view of how long it will be before the ideas begin to make money. An elementary obstacle, for example, to the progress of any new drug is approval by the various authorities, especially the American authorities. That adds years to the wait before the product can actually go on sale and generate cash, and pushes any profit prospects well into the future.

Try to assess how adequate the resources being raised will prove. Often called the 'burn', this weighs the cash available against the money consumed in research and development. Biotechnology companies especially are liable to use up cash at a ferocious rate, and may well need re-financing several times before they emerge – if they do – with a product which not only does what they hope, but which generates revenue from sales. Indeed, the odds are that any successful venture at all will need to return to shareholders for more money before it can hit the big time. No matter what the directors may say, new ventures always take longer than the promoters expect – and they will always need to raise more money.

In the New Millennium, there are many such companies in the biotechnology and pharmaceuticals business. They are almost impossible for the ordinary investor to evaluate. Try to check medical journals, look closely at the qualifications of the directors, research workers, and the sponsoring house. Such companies can be wonderfully exciting, but too many operate in a crowded, fiercely competitive market. Sadly, though some of the smaller ones look appealing, the odds are weighed against them.

The flood of internet-related companies has posed particular problems. Hardly any make profits, many have little revenue, and few have proven management. Judging them is tough. Business to business ventures look sounder than those trying to create a new market by selling to the consumer. In many cases, they will be out-muscled as existing bricks and mortar retail companies move in to providing their own internet service.

Though they have been criticised, I tend to favour some of the internet incubator funds. They invest in several different projects, and thus spread the risk. They also employ specialist managers with some skills in evaluating internet ideas, and with a sound knowledge of how to run companies. Pick the ones with the best-established names behind them, and which sell at the more modest premiums to asset value. Do not pay prices which value the company at five times the worth of assets. Try to pay no more than double — you may have to pay a premium because the investments may be in unquoted companies at cost, and hopefully they will be worth much more at some stage.

Crucially, watch out for the free float. Many of these stocks soar to a massive opening day premium because there is no stock in the market. If they issue only 5% of the shares to new investors, the price will rocket because there is a shortage of supply. Do not rush in. They will fall back. And for the longer term, watch how long the directors and their advisers are locked in. Most will not be allowed to sell their shares for one or two years. As that selling time rolls around, be careful.

There has also been a flurry of companies operating in the computer industry, either manufacturing hardware (the machines), or the software (the programmes which make them work). Again, it can be very difficult to understand what they do, or whether they are any good. Most have not been penny stocks, though there are a few. The penny stock variety should be treated with special caution if they are new issues. The tip sheet *Techinvest* is the best guide to their merits. Most of these new ventures are now coming to the stock market proper or the AIM, but there are some being touted on overseas markets. Many of the markets are of dubious standing. You may find it all too easy to buy such potential wonder shares, urged on by some eager salesman, but they may be almost impossible to sell, no matter how exciting the prospects for the company may appear. Anything listed on the Vancouver Exchange is especially dangerous, even if the shares are sometimes traded under a special London Exchange rule. Stay clear.

Sadly, in the end, you must accept that buying shares in any new venture is a gamble. The nature of the sponsors will give you a firmer idea of its plausibility than almost anything else. But it is no guarantee. Some of the City's biggest names have been lured into some of the barmiest projects yet. The boys at what was S.G. Warburg were behind Ionica, the wire-less telecoms company, which went bust in 1998 just 15 months after flotation, losing hundreds of millions in the process. And understand especially that if an exciting new venture is packaged in penny share form, it is probably done that way to attract smaller investors who may be more inclined to rush in without conducting proper research. Issuing houses are not fools – but some of them may think you are.

New Products

Spotting a money-making opportunity in a penny share with a new product is a little less perilous than backing a completely new venture. At least the whole business is not starting from scratch, and though their penny share status may indicate that they have had problems, at least the directors have some experience of running a public company. That said, this too is something of a hit-or-miss business, and whether you get involved depends largely on whether you can share the management's hopes for their new idea.

The standard guidelines apply – check the competition, the record of the directors, and the substance of the company itself to see if it has resources to support a new idea and build it into a winner. Many investors stood back from Pentland Industries, one of the market's most stunning success stories, because they were nervous of chairman Stephen Rubin's involvement on the fringe of the London & County Securities secondary banking scandal of the mid-Seventies. And it seemed improbable that a small British company could come up with something as simple as a new running shoe and outsell the giants to become one of the hottest names in American retailing. But Rubin and Pentland did it with Reebok. Anyone who backed him could have multiplied their money more than 150 times.

I confess, though, I worried about Pentland all the way up, and as a result of my fears about the London & County story, kept clear. Anyone who followed the advice I am giving here would have missed out, too. It just goes to show that there are exceptions to every rule, and there is no perfect, textbook formula for spotting winning shares.

New Issues

New issues are not the same as new ventures, thank goodness. To gain a full Stock Exchange listing, companies need a three-year record at least. A few new issues fall into the penny share class. They can be judged by the standard investment criteria – dividend yield, price earnings ratio, comparison with others in the same industry, and the strength and reputation of the sponsor – this last item is particularly important. Some low-price new issues can score penny-share-like super returns, if you are lucky.

My one significant reservation comes, however, in the similarity that exists between new issues and new ventures, and a warning I have already given above. Issuing houses have great freedom in deciding how to structure flotations. There is no particular reason why shares should be floated at a penny share price. If it happens, it is being done for a reason, perhaps because the sponsors think there may be more unsophisticated suckers playing the penny share game. They may deliberately be creating a stock which can be more open to manipulation. That may be good – they will want to manipulate it upward. It can be bad, because the real value of the business may be more suspect. Make your own judgement on how much risk you are ready to take. But be aware of the possible trap.

American Companies

UK investors tend to come across two varieties of American company – the US company which is floating over here because it is cheaper, easier, or some such thing, and the whiz-bang, hush-hush, once-in-a-lifetime offer which some villain will make you over the phone. Quite often, both may be penny stocks. Both must be treated with a scepticism which should range from extreme to total.

US companies floating here always have some plausible line. Sadly, experience suggests that nothing is convincing enough to explain why they should come to the UK instead of staying at home, where the markets are much more diverse and the potential buyers wealthier. In the end, the chances are that the companies have come to the United Kingdom because regulations will not let them float in the USA in their present state, and there may be more gullible folk to be talked into buying here. One or two of the US companies floated in London by respectable City firms have worked out fairly well. Most have been bad to disastrous. Avoid them.

The other kind of American company which is widely offered to UK investors should be avoided at all costs. It makes me furious that, time and again, dubious characters can get on the telephone, often using lists of investors who have been burnt in other speculative share scams, and persuade people to buy shares. Though the buyer may not know it, the shares are often real penny stocks. The sellers may have bought them for a fraction of a penny – a hundred for a penny in some cases. They may sell them in the UK for almost £1, maybe more.

The come-on will always be the same. Stock is available, but almost all has been sold. The vendor can let you have the last few, if you hurry. The company has some wonderful new process, as yet in the development stage and unknown to most of the competition, but sure to revolutionise the market. There are no profit figures available yet, but confidential projections speak of enormous sums. Ask for a set of accounts, or a placing document, and you will get a glossy brochure, perhaps photocopies of press cuttings saying something good, but nothing which resembles proper accounts – though it may look impressive. It would. These boys are in the business of selling illusions.

If you ask where the shares are traded, you will be told in Denver, Florida, Nevada. . . who knows? On the over-the-counter market, or Nasdaq, or the pink sheets. The salesman himself may promise you will be able to sell to his company for a big gain in a few months.

Forget it. These are simple crooks, with companies which may not actually exist, or are empty shells if they do. You will not be able to sell, though you may be told of price moves which yield enormous profits for a while. Somehow, though, you will find that you can never quite manage to sell at these inflated prices. By the time you wake up and want to sell, the price will have slumped. Or the market or salesman will have disappeared completely. Or – a favourite trick for getting more out of you – you will be given a goodish sounding price so long as you put the money into another whiz-bang stock – plus a little extra investment to sweeten it. You never see your cash back, but end up pouring more into the same hole. Never, ever, buy shares from a stranger over the phone.

Mining Companies

In my book, I am afraid, mining companies come into the extremely dangerous category. I saw the great Australian mining boom of the Sixties, met the legendary London investment heroes who backed Poseidon and saw companies selling for a few coppers soar to unbelievable heights – and plunge again. And I remember watching one share – Tasminex, I think it was – rocket from £8 to £12 in an hour one morning, only to marvel that it was £14 when I came back from lunch, and to despair on finding that it had actually touched £20 while I was chewing my steak, and had then slipped back a bit. As I recall, the boss had struck incredibly rich deposits of something or other while digging a latrine. I hardly need mention what he had really found. Gamblers who lost a fortune on Tasminex certainly formed their own conclusions about it.

To this day, I am uncertain about the truth of another Aussie classic. But I do believe I actually employed the journalist who was moonlighting on some news agency, and became involved in a touch of confusion over the mining sample figures which appeared on the tapes the next morning. By the time the correct figures were published, drastically scaling down the size of the find, several people had bought and sold the shares at a very handsome profit. My friend, who was always ready to deal in and out quickly when he saw the chance, was grinning like the Cheshire Cat for days. Perhaps he just got lucky.

Such things do not happen these days, do they? How could they? Mining stocks are well regulated, we are told. Odd, though, how many small Aussie mining share bosses do the rounds of their mates in London every so often, dropping a word or two here and there. And it must be coincidence that their mates always know when to buy and sell, and how shrewdly they anticipate company announcements. Sadly, it seems to me that even they, too, often end up losing money at it in the end.

There are splendid Australian shares, super Canadian resource stocks, and wonderfully well-informed, honest brokers on the mining scene. It may just be that I have never met them. And as for the more recently fashionable Irish mining stocks, some of which have scored wonderful profits for punters, you can scarcely wish to meet more charming fellows. It is just that they do not quite seem to attach the same meaning to words as some of the rest of us. Perhaps it is our problem.

Apply a little cold logic to much of what the mining enthusiasts have to say, and dreams sometimes turn to dust. It hardly seems to matter how careful you may be. One chum did once persuade me to back one golden Aussie opportunity. He was going to join the board, handle their finances from the London end. He had gone out there, visited the site, knew what they could do, marvelled at the quantity of amber nectar they could shift at speed. I did not lose very much, because I chickened out and sold early. I think his faith was tested when he had to sell his house later. The company still exists, I believe. I may even have a share or two. I never expect to get a penny back.

Goodness knows, it is easy enough to lose money in the UK, without tossing cash to enterprising colonial boys who see Brits as fair game. So next time someone tells you about this lovely little stock with rights slap bang next to the biggest find in the whole of the world (nickel, zinc, platinum, or some exotic metal you have never heard of), tell him to get lost. It is the oldest trick in the game. A miss in mining is as good as a mile. All that is new these days is that the marvel might be next door to some site in a land you have never heard of before, and certainly cannot pronounce, tucked away in the steppes of the former Soviet Union, or on the wildest edge of China.

Never forget, either, the sneakiest of all old Aussie tricks. A lot of British investors never will. When the shares Brits may have paid pounds for were down to a few pence, the Aussies floated rights issues. If you did not pay up in time, under Aussie rules you forfeited your shares. And you know how long it can take for documents to reach this country from Down Under.

Things may have changed, cobber. It may all be pure and clean now. But if you want to play the Aussie mining game, do it without me. You will find no encouragement in this book. The same goes for Canadian resource stocks, lifeblood to some of the world's smoothest hustlers. And as for the Russian resource boys, some of them with an Irish listing, forget it. The Russian economy may be ramshackle and backward. But those boys with snow on their boots certainly understand how a backhander here and a present there can smooth the way in a capitalist world. And if the mine should ever produce any real revenue, there will be comrades with Kalashnikovs at the door to make sure it stays in the Motherland. Make no mistake – I am not joking. I have met several of our comrades, and the tales they tell me about how it works – always with the other chap, of course – confirm that you should keep every capitalist penny safe at home, well out of their clutches.

NINE

When Not to Buy – and the Time to Sell

✸

In many ways, this is the most important section in the book. It never ceases to amaze and horrify me how little attention is paid to selling shares. Investment advisers galore say little or nothing about it. Perhaps they forget, or perhaps they hate to introduce a negative note, fearing that talking about getting out spoils the optimistic, up-beat air which accompanies the dream of buying a would-be winner. That might lose them a trade, and sacrifice their commission.

In approaching 40 years as a financial journalist, I have read thousands of letters from small investors, many telling their troubles, trying to understand how things went wrong. Over the past decade, I have been meeting more investors face to face, at exhibitions or talking at investment conferences. The strength of the stock market and the astonishing success of privatisation issues from British Telecom onwards meant most small investors enjoyed their experiences in most of the Eighties. They made money, and had fun.

Many private investors took a hammering in the Crash of October 1987, and limped along in the succeeding years. Whenever I update this book, I am relieved that I have put in warnings galore, and have never been trapped into the over-optimism of the running bull years. Above all, I always check to be sure that this chapter is written with extra care. Whatever the warnings elsewhere in the book, this is the section which carries the lessons which should save anyone who heeds them from the worst impact of any crash.

In the Eighties, I gave many warnings about the possibility of a setback in share prices. It was nothing clever. I cannot claim to have foreseen exactly when it was coming. I stopped writing my regular tipping column in the *Mail* in the summer of 1986 because I was nervous about the level of the market, and worried whether it made sense advising people to buy shares then. With the benefit of hindsight, that was too early to pull out. Indeed, though I thought the market too high in the autumn of 1987, I had expected it to rise a little further before falling – and never imagined it would plummet so dramatically. Through the years, some gloomsters made a comfortable living frightening the wits out of investors, predicting a dramatic slump. They must have cost their followers a fortune in lost profit opportunities, keeping them out when the market was on the rise.

They knew, as we all should, that eventually their warnings would be right. The market does not go on rising forever. Slump always follows boom. And vice versa. But if you are too timid, you never get in there to make the money, to play the game, in the good times.

Once you are in the market, what matters is not whether you can predict the slump, but whether you get caught when it comes. The beauty of playing the share game is that though no-one can cover every trap and dodge every setback, you can cut your losses. You can usually ensure that you do not lose everything. It is up to you. If you are awake, you should be able to make sure you come out with a fair chunk of your profits intact.

That is why this section of the book is vitally important. It is a shame, in a way, that it comes so near the end. Logic demands it. There is no point in talking about selling before you have found something to buy. But until you have actually sold your winning shares, and popped the money into your pocket, you have not made a profit. Paper profits do not count. They buy you nothing, and could vanish overnight. The only profits which matter are the ones you pocket – never forget it.

The slump of 1973 and 1974 wiped millions of pounds off stock market fortunes. Even Jim Slater, the share genius of his generation, ended up a minus millionaire. His friends helped stake him to start again, and he has done very well indeed. But even for someone as shrewd as him, the crash of the Seventies was more than wipe-out. It was over-kill. That should not happen to you.

In the wake of the Crash of 1987, similar problems occurred. Individual traders galore were wiped out, left with debts they never could meet. Companies which survived the initial impact gradually lost the battle in the months and years which followed. Houses, cars, yachts were sold, children taken out of private schools, and marriages collapsed. A few unfortunates committed suicide. Even well into the Nineties, large punters were still shaking, several clinging on, desperately hoping a stock market boom would magically save them from losses finally coming home from the Lloyd's insurance market.

That is no way to be. It is dismal, dreadful stuff, a terrible punishment for growing too greedy. Many of them may have been saved, finally, by the great bull market through the mid-Nineties, just so long as they sold before it began to turn bad again. And if they had not borrowed too heavily to finance their come-back.

Never Borrow to Buy

That points up the first, elementary lesson of when not to buy shares. Do not buy if you cannot afford it. Only use money you can afford to lose. Whatever happens, do not buy if you have to borrow.

No matter how heavily the early passages of this book have emphasised that you should only play with money you can afford to lose, some will ignore it. Others will see the sense of it, but get carried away. Many of us sometimes feel we carry a lucky charm, that the worst only happens to someone else. We could never lose the lot ourselves. Not us. That is the danger. Taste a little success in the penny share game, and you could really be in trouble. The day you make your first killing is the most dangerous of your investing career. Amid the elation, you grow more confident. You have done it once, why not again? It was not that difficult, after all. This stock market business seems easy, now you know how.

The attitude is understandable. I know. I felt that way once, years ago. You forget the problems, the worries you faced along the way. It all turned out well, in the end. After the first winner, it is easy to get careless, to neglect some of the checks you perhaps should have made. Someone tells you about a good thing. Maybe they got it right before. It must be worth having a go. . .

Think like that, and you could be on the way to learning a nasty lesson. You could be limbering up to lose a lot of the money you made on your first winner. Worse, you could be on the way to thinking you have found something so good that you ought to put a bit more into it. Perhaps you can use the cash you had stacked away for that rainy day? You will be able to put it back when you have made your next profit, surely. Or perhaps the cash you set aside for the phone bill, or the holiday? Or what about that small overdraft you took out for a week or two for some new issue? Maybe you could stretch that for a few weeks? Or delay paying off your Barclaycard or Access bill. You could just pay back the minimum, and let the loan run on for a month or two – just until this latest share takes off.

Do not do it. It is fatal. You will end up in debt, and in trouble. The stock market is far too risky to play that way. Never think it will not happen to you, that you will be fine, you will get away with it – that you are onto a winner, for sure.

If I seem to be labouring the point unduly – good. You, at least, have got the message. Believe me, I have been horrified to chat with apparently level-headed investors, who clearly knew their way around the market, only to have them confide in me that they were planning to take out a 'little loan' to play, or that they were between houses, and would use the money they had set aside for a deposit – just for a month or two. . . Madness. Do not get sucked in.

Gossip

Time and again, commentators hold forth about the foolishness of listening to gossip, buying on a tip from a chum, someone you meet in a pub, or a neighbour. People do it. Sometimes it works. Sometimes you hit lucky. And that is why it pays to try to check out gossip. By all means listen. But never deal, never go blind, without trying to make sense of what you hear.

If your informant really knows something sensational, enough to guarantee a winner, he is an insider. For him to tell you is illegal. For you to buy is illegal. If he works for the company or their advisers, or has some other official connection, and is giving you advance information about something he knows is happening, he is passing on inside information. Both of you could end up in prison if you are caught. Surveillance is getting sharper, the rules are getting tougher. If you are an ordinary, unsophisticated investor, the chances of being prosecuted and getting a stiff sentence are much greater than if you are some City slicker, who knows better how to hide the deal, and can afford some smart lawyer to argue the odds.

Realise, too, that people who work for a company are not always the best judge of what things mean for a share price, even if they are directors. They may be giving you perfectly accurate information, and information which is not fully covered by insider trading rules. Who can quarrel with the foreman who knows that extra machines have been installed, and work is flooding in? It is only natural that he should be pleased and mention it to a few mates.

Apply that knowledge to share trading, however, and though the news may be right, it may mean nothing. The City may know already. It may have sent the shares up months ago, when the company announced it had won the order. If extra production lines are going in, broking analysts will probably know already. So there is no point in buying the shares.

What, though, if you should hear there is an exciting new product on the way? Who knows? Perhaps it will make a big difference. Maybe the City has not heard. Or what if the works have been crawling with chaps from another company, or some well-known industrialist visited the factory? Who knows what might be afoot? It is hardly insider information when it comes from a charge-hand with an ear for gossip. It might mean something. So do not ignore it. But do not necessarily place too much faith in it. Check.

Similar thoughts apply to tit-bits your broker may drop your way. If he really knows something, he cannot tell you. A penny share punter is unlikely to be first in line for his choicest information. He may simply want you to think he is trying to help, or he may have a few shares to sell for himself or a friend. Perhaps he may have spotted a good opportunity, and he may be putting his clients in while he sees the chance. Be careful, but do not ignore him. Gossip can be good. You never quite know. Sometimes you can collect bits and pieces which suddenly slot into place to give you something which makes sense.

A Falling Market

Never buy in a falling market. That rule gets trotted out every so often. It makes some sense. But a shrewd investor might see a falling market as the ideal time to pick up stock unnoticed.

It is a matter of degree. The penny punter will not be able to dictate the course of a share price, pushing it up or down by sheer weight of money. In a major market turn, there is no point spitting into the wind. Unfortunately, it is not easy to decide whether you are in a great grizzly bear market, or simply seeing a setback which might be over soon and so presents a buying opportunity.

Unless there is a clearly defined event which changes things – like our exit from the Exchange Rate Mechanism in autumn 1992, or the Crash of October 1987 – try to judge the climate from the overall press comment over a reasonable period, three months, perhaps. Waiting that long may mean you suffer a substantial setback before you do anything. Such decisions are not comfortable. But cast your mind back six months. If you are honest, you may be able to recall that the climate seemed completely different then. It is amazing how things change, imperceptibly day by day. With the benefit of time and hindsight, you can then see how radical that tiny daily change eventually turned out to be.

If you are in regular touch with the market, you know moods can change dramatically. And change again, before long. Spotting a major sustained switch is not simple. People who claim to hit it on the button are fooling themselves, and should make the most of their luck while it lasts.

Nonetheless, it is possible to measure the general temperature. If it feels uncertain, hold off. You may not lose much by waiting, and you will feel happier for it. There are times when it is best to stay away, no matter how eagerly you want action. There are almost always a few shares which make money, even in the nastiest market. But the odds are loaded heavily against you finding them. If in doubt, stay out.

Reading the Share Price

If shares sometimes shout "Buy" to those who are listening, they can also sound a warning. A falling price on days when all others are rising gives a clear message. So, too, does an unexpectedly small rise after what might appear to be good figures. Someone doubts what they have seen, or expected much better. Other prices simply drift back, losing a penny or two, holding steady, then drifting off again. Beware. This is no time to buy.

Far better to hold off, watch for the price to establish a bottom and then begin to move up. It never hurts to give someone else the first 10%, or the last 10% at the top. What matters is taking the big piece in the middle. Someone always knows more than you. Let them take the biggest risk.

Equally, the signs which make you hesitate over buying may be the first warning that you should consider selling if you hold the stock. If shares are not rising, they may simply drift off through lack of interest. Or if they merely hold steady when others all around are going up, perhaps some insider is taking profits, and that is what is halting the rise. Think about it.

Price moves tend to go to extremes – too high, or too low. If you spot that special bargain, and it carries on getting cheaper, let it settle. It may not mean anything is wrong as it continues to fall. There may be a big seller, needing cash for some reason, steadily dribbling out shares as the market will take them. Let him finish. Make sure the tap is turned off before you come in. Be patient, and let the price bounce off the bottom and settle awhile, making sure the selling really is over. A good broker can sometimes give you a good idea of how it goes.

Late News

One of the few absolutely unambiguous rules is that late news is bad news. Never ignore it. Bad profits always seem to take longer to add up than good ones. It is not always easy to check, but most companies report their interim and annual profits at roughly the same time each year, unless they have announced a change in their accounting year-end.

Try to be aware of the likely reporting dates for any share which interests you. The Exchange Telegraph card shows the previous year's dates. So does the monthly *Stock Exchange Investment List* given out by some brokers. Newspapers report a table of figures expected in the week ahead, sometimes based on firm announcements by companies, sometimes guided by the previous year's custom.

A week or two of slippage may not mean any harm, though you should begin to wonder. Anything over three weeks is suspicious, unless there is a clear reason. Ask your broker about the delay, listen to what the market whispers say, and watch the share price carefully. Or ring the company secretary and ask what is happening. Never buy before you know – and think about selling the shares you may already hold.

The Time to Sell

Judging when to sell is extremely difficult. It can be as much an emotional decision as a financial one. You do grow attached to shares. They become old friends. Watch closely enough for long enough, and you begin to feel you know every move they make. Especially if you are in a winner, a friend which has made you money, and, above all – proved you right.

It is no good fooling yourself. Investment is every bit as much about ego as making money. No matter what else may be debatable, no one can argue with the figures. If you bought at 10p and sold at 20p, you were right. . . but only if you actually sold, took that profit for real, instead of just in your mind.

Cutting Your Losses

The one clear, basic, unbreakable rule is to let your profits run and to cut your losses quickly. It is so clear, so simple, so absolutely obvious. Yet so many investors ignore it.

Never mind that selling at a loss is a confession that you got it wrong. That does not matter. Everyone gets it wrong sometimes. The smart investor is the one who gets it right six times out of ten. The one who gets it right ten out of ten is a liar. The smart investor is the one who acts before the losers become an embarrassment, before they cost too much money.

Think about it. If you buy five shares and make it a firm rule to sell any which fall by 25%, you only need one of your five to double, and you still have not lost money even if all of the other four fall by 25%. If you do better, and two of your five double and you sell the other three at a 25% loss, you will have an overall gain of 25%. An investment of £1,000 in each would have yielded a profit of £1,250, even though you got three out of five wrong.

Selling losers quickly makes so much sense. You may never pick a share which doubles – there are no guarantees. But you need never hold one which halves. The choice is yours. You can always – or almost always – sell on the way down and limit your loss. Choose how much you want to lose.

It is unusual for a share to fall by half in one move, or to be suspended and become worthless before shareholders have a chance to sell. It happens, of course. But you would be very unlucky or foolish to buy the day before it happens, to get no warning at all. Punting in penny shares is a form of gambling, but a relatively attractive one because you can exercise significant control over the size of your losses. You can sell when you see they are mounting too high.

So do it, please. Choose your own limits. But do set some limits, and set them when you start. No one buys a share with the intention of losing money. Prudent investors are aware of the possibility, and face up to it by resolving to sell if the price should fall to a particular point, and by fixing that point when they buy. A 25% fall is not a bad limit, although it is not inflexible. Some penny shares are too volatile for a 25% margin to work properly, especially on very low-priced stocks. Given the extra risk involved, it may be sensible to set a limit of up to 50% before you exit.

The Stop-Loss System

In all of my investment books, I advocate using a stop-loss system. It can be applied to penny shares, and I recommend it strongly, but with a variation or two. There is no mystery to it. When you buy a share, set a price at which you will sell should things go wrong and the price falls. If you set it 20% below the price you pay, that means you would sell if a 50p share fell to 40p – automatically, without hesitation.

A few brokers will operate the system for you. Most will not. You need to track the price yourself, and tell the broker when to sell. In a falling market, you might not get out at exactly the price you intend. Never mind. Do it regardless. Never lower the stop-loss point. Never give yourself an excuse to wriggle around it. The idea is to impose an automatic discipline on your dealings. Believe me, most investors need it. It is amazing how often people cling to losers, making excuses, hoping they will come right. Often they sell winners to carry the cripples.

With penny shares, a 20% fall may not allow enough room for manoeuvre. You may find yourself selling almost as soon as you have bought. The limit must be a matter for individual judgement. Decide how much of a loss you are prepared to take. Remember that the middle price will conceal quite a margin between the actual buying and selling price. And that dealing costs are proportionately heavier on a penny share. So when it comes, the actual loss will almost certainly be larger than you had anticipated.

A limit between 25% and 30% below the price you paid seems sensible for most penny shares. If a share has fallen that much, something is almost certainly badly wrong. It is just that you do not know what it is. You do not want to tie up money in a dud. You are not just losing the cash in that share – but are losing the profit you might be making if it was in a share which was going up.

That said, penny shares are different. In a strong market, almost anything gets picked up sooner or later. Few companies are allowed to go to the wall. There is almost always someone who is ready to pay a premium to buy into a dud company, just for the share quotation. The dogged penny punter, then, can claim it is worth hanging on, no matter what happens. That is an attitude I would deplore in other circumstances. It reeks of folly, even in a penny share. But if you do want to hang on and accept the risks of behaving with a bone-headed stubbornness, it might just be pardonable in a penny share in a bull market. But only just. The sensible investor will be more flexible, and more decisive.

Taking Profits

The stop-loss system is not merely designed to contain losses. It also provides an invaluable aid to taking profits. Once again, wider margins may be applied to penny shares than to more conventional investments. But the basics hold good for both.

Once you have set your stop-loss price, move it up as the share rises. And keep it moving up, not down. That way, you build the profit you will take once your winner turns down. Say you buy at 50p, and set the stop-loss at 37.5p, a 25% margin. If your share rises 5p to 55p, move your stop-loss point up by 5p to 42.5p. And so on. At 62.5p, your stop-loss price should be 50p, so you are breaking even, before costs.

If you should hit 80p, the stop-loss point should be up to 67.5p. Then, even if your winner begins to slip, you will be using the system to sell at a profit, locking in a gain of 17.5p before expenses by selling when the price falls to 67.5p. You will not have sold at the top, but you will not have lost all of your profit, even if the market really is in decline.

Clearly the system calls for common sense. The one inflexible rule is that you do not lower your stop-loss point once you have set it. If you are not an aggressive trader, you may choose, however, to raise it less rapidly when a share takes off. Frequently penny shares enjoy a great surge, then slip back quite sharply in a bout of profit-taking. If you are an aggressive trader, you might shift your stop-loss up at once. Otherwise, it might be as well to let that subside before you adjust your stop-loss. If, for example, the share you bought at 50p jogs along to 62.5p, then rockets to 100p on news of a deal, you may not want to bang your stop-loss up to 87.5p immediately. You might see the share fall back through that in a day or two, as short-term traders jump out.

You might prefer to wait a week or two, see where the price settles, then shift the stop-loss higher. If, say, the share settles at 85p, a 12.5p margin might not suit you. You may not want to risk being taken out of a potential high-flyer on a relatively modest setback. But do not abandon the system altogether. Shift the stop-loss point to, say, 65p, or 67.5p.

It is important to realise that you can afford to take a more relaxed view of winners, but not of losers. You want to stay with a winner as long as you reasonably can. You want to be out of a loser as quickly and painlessly as possible.

The stop-loss system is not infallible. It means you never sell at the absolute top. And it will take you out of some high-flyers too soon. Some temporary blip may trigger a stop-loss and cause you to sell early, leaving you cursing when all comes right again and the price leaps. Selling a winner too quickly seems to upset investors more than backing a loser. But no system is perfect. Hard experience tells me that the stop-loss works. It helps you stay with the winners, and cut your losses sensibly.

Selling Half

There is a popular notion that you should sell half of your holding whenever a share doubles. One of the penny share tip sheets is fond of it. Superficially, it sounds attractive. It allows you to retrieve your original investment stake, and use it elsewhere. The shares you keep have then effectively cost you nothing, so you can afford to take a risk, and sit with them whatever happens. Once you have sold half, the rest is pure profit.

I do not approve of this. Picking penny share winners is tough enough without selling them too soon. The lists of top performers are not crammed with shares which have doubled. The real winners have multiplied five, six, seven times over. The dream stocks soar one hundred-fold. Why sell just because you are on to a good thing?

Think about it. If you had put £500 into Polly Peck at 20p, and sold half at 40p, how would you have felt when it reached 400p? At 400p, your £500 stake would have been worth £10,000 if you had kept the lot. If you had sold half at 40p, you would have had £5,500. The difference is enormous. It would still be enormous, no matter how many other winners you picked with the £500 you took out of Polly at 40p – not to mention how much you would have made if you were still holding them all when Polly went to £30.

Try the stop-loss system instead of selling half. It is prudent to think about taking profits whenever you score a big winner. But it is much more rewarding to ride a winner all the way up, and to sell when the excitement begins to fade. A stop-loss system would have taken you out of Polly long before it hit real trouble.

And ask yourself why you are punting penny shares to start with? Merely to double your money? Or to chase the dream, the really big killing?

The Standard Rules

The big penny share winners will move way out of their class and become established as serious companies, analysed by stockbrokers galore, bought by the big institutions, and watched every inch of the way by the City. Super. That is just what you want. The more widely the stock becomes accepted, the more buyers will come in, and the bigger the profit for the original punter.

At that stage, however, more conventional standards begin to take over. The stop-loss system still holds good. But there are other factors to think about in timing a sale. It is a good idea, for instance, to step back every so often, gather what information you can from stockbrokers' circulars, newspapers and magazines, and look at the rating of your investment. Ask yourself if you would buy it at the present price if you were stumbling upon it for the first time.

Look at the dividend yield and the price earnings ratio – historic and prospective – and compare them to similar companies. Does your winner still look good value? Or is it too far ahead of the game? Allow a premium for the dynamic growth which has taken it from penny share to middle-range investment. Has the management settled for more modest growth in future? Or is it still ambitious, eager to make more money for everyone – and fast? Are the signs of corporate middle age creeping in? Are directors selling shares? Perhaps you ought to be lightening your load, and plunging back into some penny punt.

If your penny winner is a recovery share or a cyclical stock, look out for the competition. How are others in the industry faring? Have they begun to report that growth is slowing? How are companies further along the production chain doing? If house sales are falling, will that hit your brick maker? If the pound is slipping, will that make raw materials more expensive, and eat into margins? What a worry this share punting business can be.

The Economy

Tempting as it may be, you cannot ignore the economy. Higher interest rates mean heavier borrowing costs, which is especially serious if you are in a smaller company which is struggling with hefty loans, waiting for a recovery in trade. The more expensive money is, the slower the general pick-up in business will be. The weaker the pound, the greater the pressure to push interest rates up, and the more expensive the cost of buying anything from abroad, be it clothes for your retailer to sell, or timber for your housebuilder. A weaker pound will help exporters, however, making their goods look cheap overseas.

Then there is oil. Cheap oil helps industry, reduces the cost of the energy which everyone uses, but undermines the value of the pound because the North Sea makes sterling something of a petro-currency. Expensive oil raises costs, cuts profit margins, boosts the pound and adds to the pressure on inflation. In fact, in the Nineties, the steady slide in the oil price has been a great benefit in holding down inflation, giving our economy a boost which is often overlooked.

Assessing the economy in detail is vastly complicated – the Chancellor and the Treasury get it wrong, time and again. All the penny share player needs to heed is the crude direction of the main economic moves. The cost of money is probably most crucial for penny shares. Lower interest rates are good news for almost all, and mean the economy is doing well, or poised to recover. Cheap money keeps the stock market cheerful. Leave the details to the economists – but, as in any market, be very wary if the picture is getting gloomier. That might well be the stage at which to say goodbye to penny shares, perhaps for a few years, until brighter signs begin to appear.

The Day to Sell

If you do decide that it is nearly time to sell, spare a thought for the day you do it. The stock market is about anticipation. It looks ahead. That is why shares often fall on good news. The market was expecting it, and needed something supercharged to mark shares higher. Short-term players buy in a few days ahead of profit news, anticipating a rise. They sell as the figures are announced – or just before. If you hold a share which is due to make an announcement, it often pays to sell just before it comes, rather than just after, unless you are so confident of really good news that you will not want to sell whatever happens in the short term.

Thursday or Friday were not generally good days to sell when the old Stock Exchange account system used to operate. Now they matter less, unless you are in an all-action share. The *Investors Chronicle* appears on Friday morning. It usually carries a flurry of recommendations, and might move prices higher at once. Many do not see it until Friday evening, so there is some carry over of buying on the following Monday. And the Sunday papers tend to scatter tips around in shot-gun style, hoping to hit something which will move. Much of it might be irresponsible, public-relations inspired rubbish, emphasising the positive and overlooking any down-side, sometimes written by journalists who boast they have never bought a share in their life. But it can shift prices and give your share an unexpected bonus when dealings open on Monday morning. Some of the most influential tip sheets also reach subscribers at the weekend, so they tend to buy early in the week. It means that Monday or Tuesday might be better days to sell than Thursday or Friday.

Sell in May

'Sell in May' is the most widely quoted of the old stock market saws. In the mid-Eighties, it began to establish quite a grip. But in 1987, the announcement of the General Election date sent shares soaring. The smarter players, who had sold in April ahead of what looked as if it might be a May exodus, were left in the cold as prices leapt. And in 1995, prices shook off nerves about interest rate rises, and happily followed Wall Street up.

It does tend to work more often than not, however. The City grows quieter from the end of May until late in August. The big names drift away on holiday, or pop off to Ascot, Wimbledon, Henley, or the cricket. Fewer deals are done, and the tempo drops until September rolls around.

But there is money to be made at any time of the year. December and

January tend to be better than average months to buy. Somehow, the New Year seems to inspire optimism. We always manage to persuade ourselves that things must be better by the end of the year, so buying early makes sense.

Tax

Tax is an also-ran. Do not let it influence your investment decisions. In the 1999 tax year, you can take capital gains, man and wife, of up to £6,800 each before tax is chargeable at your top rate. There is no tax on gains until you actually sell and realise them.

Gains tax is not too much of a burden for the small investor. If you are doing really well, you may prefer to take some gains in one tax year to exploit the full amount of your exemption. Or postpone taking gains until the next tax year begins. Ask your broker what is best.

It also makes sense to use the tax-free option of an Individual Savings Account, as mentioned earlier. But it is a mistake to let tax planning dominate your investment strategy. Worry about making the gains first.

Words of Warning

Playing penny shares is a high-risk business. Do not get sucked in too deep. Once your name starts appearing on share registers, or as a subscriber to tip sheets, you may receive all manner of investment propositions through the post. Never take any of them up without first taking advice.

Never part with a penny if you are approached by telephone. The friendly fellow who wants to do you a favour only wants your money.

Never be tempted into any form of investment in commodities, futures, options, or overseas shares. You will lose in the end.

Never sign any agreement saying you understand the risks unless you really do understand how the scheme works, and what those risks may be.

Never trust the so-called professional who answers your queries with assurances that he knows how it is done, you can leave it to him. He will end up with your money.

The instant your penny share punting starts to worry you, pull out. Once investment ceases to be fun, forget it.

If you do have problems, and if you are worried about some dodgy scheme or share pusher, by all means e-mail me through my website. I take such things very seriously. Even if I cannot help you, I may be able to help others escape the trap. Please, though, accept my apologies in advance if I do not answer letters. I always intend to, but often the pressure of work is such that I do not get round to it. But I always take notice.

Good luck.